The Entrepreneur Lifestyle

Starting Lean, Working for Yourself, and Going from Struggle to Success in a Business of Your Own

Chris Lutz

Copyright © 2014 Chris Lutz

All rights reserved.

ISBN: 1502966824
ISBN-13: 978-1502966827

WHY YOU SHOULD BUY THIS BOOK!

- Because you're an entrepreneur and would like help and support in that journey.

- You want to become an entrepreneur.

- You're interested in inspiring stories and motivation from people like you.

- You'd like to be more organized.

- You'd like to make more money.

- You'd like to quit your current job.

- You want more freedom.

DEDICATION

I dedicate this book to my Mom and Dad for giving me a good start in life to pursue what I wanted and make the most of it. Any other set of circumstances and I may not have been able to do and be who I am. I'm forever indebted to them.

CONTENTS

Acknowledgments

    Introduction   1

1. **The Why: What is your Philosophy in life?**   3
2. **A Special Class of People**   8
3. **Corporate Fallacies**   10
4. **How Most People Live**   13
5. **It's Your Nature**   16
6. **American Entrepreneurial History**   19
7. **The How: Deciding What You Want**   21
8. **Struggle in the Lean Times**   23
9. **Fatigue, Persistence, and Your Will**   24
10. **Getting Organized**   38
11. **Sales and Marketing**   44
12. **Operations**   66
13. **Finance**   87
14. **Growth and Conveying Your Vision to Others**   141
15. **Exit, Life Cycle, End Game**   147
16. **Putting it all Together**   150

ACKNOWLEDGMENTS

I'd like to acknowledge all of my entrepreneur friends who continually impress and inspire me to keep pushing forward on the journey.

INTRODUCTION

I want to take just a minute here to express how I feel from my heart and why I wrote this book. But, first, let me give you a little back story on who I am. I've always known since I was a teenager that I wanted to start my own business. I didn't know how, but it was clearly an option. I remember having a subscription to 4Wheeler magazine as a kid and thinking how cool it would be to grow up, own property, and build a Jeep trail on it people could come and have fun on for a fee. You probably had similar ideas as a kid. I wasn't a great student. That seems to be common among entrepreneurs. However, I did excel in sports marketing and aced advanced marketing in high school. I even kept papers from those classes about entrepreneurship because I knew I'd need them one day. I still have them in a folder right here in my desk.

I had trouble reading in school. I thought I just didn't like it. As it turns out, I just can't or don't really like to read fiction. But, the one book I blew right through with no trouble at all was one I read in that same advanced marketing class. It was Harvey Mackay's Swim with the Sharks without Being Eaten Alive. Who would have thought a business book would have been the easiest thing to read for me. It really lit a fire in me. I wasn't in those clubs or groups like DECA or Future Business Leaders of America. I didn't even know how to get into them. I don't think I would have fit in anyway even though I was probably of the same mind as those kids.

During college I got into the health and fitness industry and that suited me perfectly due to the hours and what I could make for my time. It also worked because it was largely a self-driven field and I had a lot of autonomy. I've since cultivated my entrepreneurial spirit and expanded my efforts out into outdoor ventures and business to business offerings for other entrepreneurs, like this book. I have a hand in a few things. I want to take all of my passions and turn them into businesses. Perhaps you can relate.

That's a little about me, but back to you.

I just want to say that I know you. Even though I may not have met you, I probably know who you are, what your character is like, and what you're about. If you're an entrepreneur, you're like me. It's something that is in you, a part of your soul. Some people can learn what is necessary to do it, but a LOT of it is inborn as part of us, I believe. It can't be taught or learned. The unlimited persistence, the eternal optimism, the incredible stubbornness, it's all there.

But, sometimes, there's also the mental anguish. Entrepreneurs pay a price. I know you struggle. I know you don't sleep. I know you don't like routine. I know you're fiercely independent which sometimes isolates you. I know you have a million ideas running through your head all the time. Many of those things are exhausting to us, but we wouldn't have it any other way, would we?

I want to tell you that you're special. You are what made this country so great. Sadly, we are now in the minority it seems. And worse, it's getting harder to take the risks necessary to bring our ideas and vision to fruition. But, it can be done. You are incredibly tough. I know you don't seek stability or security because you know they don't really exist anyway. But, you're a hero for doing so. Literally a hero! I believe it will be us that continues to strengthen our economy and make it great again and keep it there. Not some special government program or a new President. It's you. You are on the front lines, in the field, actually making things happen when others are afraid to or too lazy to.

I want you to know that I feel the same way you do. I'm here to support you. I want you to know that I have a massive amount of respect for you, your efforts to date, and anything you attempt in the future if you're an entrepreneur. Make no mistake about it, you're part of a special club. I'm honored to be a part of that with you. Don't ever give up, don't get complacent, and continue to put your best efforts forward. You may not get all the recognition you deserve (I'm doing my best to offer you a little of it here), but that's not really why we do what we do anyway, is it?

I just simply want to say thank you for all that you do!

1 THE WHY: WHAT IS YOUR PHILOSOPHY IN LIFE?

We entrepreneurs are a special bunch, aren't we. The more I read, the more impressed, inspired and in awe I am of what some people have accomplished. Nothing against our global neighbors and friends, but especially the American risk takers. It seems America has a unique combination of environment, heritage, culture, and attitude making it the ripest place on Earth for entrepreneurship.

In the introduction, I mentioned that in high school I read a business book by Harvey Mackay. From then on I knew I wanted to be an entrepreneur. I've since had the good fortune of co-authoring this business book so that others can learn from my experience. This is the fulfillment of a dream. Read on and open your mind to the possibilities of a different kind of work life.

Many Americans have been making a huge mistake for decades. We've bought into things that others have told us about without verifying facts or thinking critically. We have had unrealistic expectations. We have some degree of narcissism. And we have become entitled. Rarely do we see alternative ways of doing things when, in fact, there are probably an infinite number of paths to our destinations.

Worst of all, as a culmination of all those factors, we've become part of the "working dead." Those are the people who trudge to work every day in a zombie-like state and continue on that path for years. Some never awaken from this state.

That's the awesome power of a culture; the ability to perpetuate itself without active interference, whether it be a business culture or the American culture as a whole. Just think, how can a company afford to pay a pension to employees who have worked for 30 or 40 years, or more? Pretty soon, the company will be paying more people who are NOT working for them than people who ARE. Do you see the flaw in this system?

Nowadays, with people living longer, it doesn't take much to eat up a lot of money quickly. Following the disastrous effects of the global financial crises and several years of recession, many may need to live without the pension that was expected to fund them for the last decades of their lives. This applies to both public and private sectors. You can't trust anybody but yourself.

Yes, it's good to specialize in a profession, but consider this for a moment: few would ever invest even a single dollar without "diversifying" it. Why, then, do we do exactly the opposite with our regular income which may be more important to our short term stability? If you're spending your whole life working for someone else for a fraction of the revenue and a vision that is not your own, you're paddling against the current. You're helping to enrich others. That's not a terrible thing, but consider a job where you could take more ownership of the end product and reap more of the benefit.

My Backstory

I've I wanted to be an entrepreneur since I was about 12 years old. It's not always this clear so early for others. I tried to follow the conventional wisdom and advice of that era; go to school, graduate, get a good job, and save for retirement. That might be good for some and things may have worked well under that formula for decades. But it's dead now!

Here's another problem: I get bored easily. I could not imagine having the same job for 10, 20, 30, or 40 years. Usually, over two to five years, I feel like I've got a really good handle on something and look for more challenges.

I have also never felt comfortable working for others. It wasn't that I was a bad employee. I may have been better than others because I understood both sides of the situation. I just sort of had this underlying feeling of guilt, for lack of a better description. I knew I was being paid and I knew I had to hustle, but it was always for somebody else, not necessarily in line with my interests. On the contrary, I'm usually a good networker and producer and can collaborate well, it just has to be in the right environment for me. I'm not a great manager though as I often expect co-workers to be like me. I have trouble recognizing and isolating the motivations of others.

Decisive and fast are my catch-words. I'm eternally optimistic; things don't bother me even when they should. Big pictures are easy but I have trouble with details. I'm working on that. These are classic entrepreneurial traits that I've found and seen in others to whom I relate.

When I was younger and played sports, I was a fairly good at ice hockey and went as far as I could in our local area. Every kid likes to think they would make it to the professional league of their sport. Of course, I wanted to make it to the NHL, however unlikely it was. In my early teens I specifically remember my Dad saying to me: "Why play when you can own the team?"

He explained that although the players got all the on-ice glory, it was the owners of the professional teams who really did well. And if I thought pro players made a lot of money, the owners made exponentially more. I didn't fully understand that at first, but what he said resonated with me. If nothing else, it was certainly an easier approach; easier on the body rather than a full-time job in a full contact sport where injuries and fist fights are a daily occurrence.

I wasn't an exceptional school student. I was slightly above average which I believe is characteristic of a lot of entrepreneurs. There were flashes of brilliance when the right things came together. I thought I didn't like reading in school. Now, I can read a book a week. It just so happened that what I was forced to read didn't match my interests or passions.

In fictional stories I find it difficult to visualize plot movements and often get lost. However, in high school, I was drawn to a sports marketing class. Having previously considered a career in Public Relations, or ideally, representing players as a sports agent, I was interested in the course. I even interviewed the parent of a teammate who was an agent for a professional player. That class held my attention. It was a prerequisite for an advanced marketing class I took as a senior in high school. I did very well in this class which offered me the opportunity to read something I would enjoy immensely, and more importantly, learn a lot from. It was Harvey Mackay's _Swim with the Sharks Without Being Eaten Alive: Outsell, Outmanage, Outmotivate, and Outnegotiate Your Competition_. I LOVED that book and still do.

That was in 1996 and I still get his weekly emails. From that single book I learned a ton about management techniques, negotiation (everything is negotiable), and how to make an unexciting business – like envelopes and paper – stand out. Mostly, though, I learned more about myself. Entrepreneurship was my likely destiny.

I held several jobs while in high school, through college, and after I graduated which allowed me to gain valuable experience and move into leadership roles. Although not a control freak, I typically like to work alone and have a lot of ideas and energy. I hate to be confined. I like to move fast and get things done quickly.

As someone else's employee I am not able to manage the power in the relationship. In fact, I disagree – massively – with the traditional American way firms are organized and run.

With someone else in charge of my efforts, direction, and, most importantly, my pay, I was uncomfortable and unhappy in the past. In fact, in my last "employed" job early in the new millennium, my pay changed drastically three times in three years. My income was wildly out of my control. I understood the need for it to change due to business conditions, but I couldn't plan ahead and had no financial regularity whatsoever that I could control.

I'm fine without regular income, as long as I can do something to change my circumstances. I've never had a salary because I was always working on commission. I didn't want a salary. My concern was always the potential upside or how much commission I could make as a direct result of my efforts. In the second year of my "employed" job, I had to work about 25 per cent more to make just under what I had made the previous year. Client appointments were at the client's mercy so it wasn't like I worked 10 or 12 hours straight all the time, although it was possible. Sometimes appointments were spread from 5 am or 6 am all the way through 8 pm or 8.30 pm. Some Mondays I came in and had 26 half hour appointments scheduled straight through the day.

Typically, I saw clients in the early morning, for a few hours in the middle of the day, and from afternoon into the late evening. That's how it was. Obviously, this burned me out.

With some control over my schedule I tried to optimize it as best I could. Despite holding a management position I was also handling most of the client appointments – often up to 90 a week. I couldn't do both and I couldn't cut back on my own appointments because my management pay was changed. As I had no problem securing new client referrals I suggested to my boss that I work straight through from 6 am to 3 pm each day – a nine-hour day plus half a day on Saturday.

He said: "Well, you kind of need to be here for the busy evenings." It was clear that the only goal was to get more clients. No matter how many clients we had, it was never enough.

I did have some vacation days. It was two weeks at first then went down to 9. I'd take a few days throughout the year and a couple of years I took off about 6 days around Christmas time because I had to use or lose them. That spurred another response. "You know, it's really difficult on us when you take all of your vacation at one time." Because one day vacations are great and will certainly keep an employee working more than full time from burning out. Some people don't get vacation at all. Work doesn't care what day it is or that you're tired. I get that. But, the point is that I couldn't do anything to better my situation. I was spinning my wheels mostly.

A typical day for me would sometimes then stretch to 13 or 14 hours. So the following year it was either continue to burn out or work more reasonable hours. The latter meant nearly a $20,000 pay cut, excluding management pay. On this commission-only job I was paid $30 an hour which, although a reasonable rate, necessitated about 90 client sessions a week just to cover expenses. Keep in mind, this was Loudoun County, Virginia, then the highest median income county in the nation at $115,500 a year per household. I knew of competitors working for themselves down the street who charged $60 to $100 an hour for the same service in less well-off areas.

In early to mid-2000 I also had other business interests so I started cultivating some of them. One was a fishing lure side business I wanted to start with my father. It centered around an ecommerce website. One day a co-worker warned that my boss thought I was spending time on that at the expense of my job.

My co-worker, in the same financial situation as me, explained on my behalf: "Well, he has to supplement his income." Why? Because our pay rates changed three times in three years.

That was a turning point. I had no power over my own pay even though I was working more than ever. Worse, it was apparently not unreasonable to dedicate outlandish hours to pursuing clients. I realized I couldn't centralize that earning power with someone else or an organization that wasn't mine.

This type of job was not for me. It would cost me the time I wanted to devote to many other interests. My life had become working long hours, going home, stuffing my face with food, going immediately to bed and going right back to work in the early morning. I needed to be in control of my time, or at least have some recourse if things didn't go the way I liked. I was in business to make something work on its own, not keep piling more on my own plate. If I felt like I was building toward something better, I would have been ok, but it felt more and more like I was struggling to tread water. The owner wasn't really making anything, my and other's pay was steadily going down, yet we had more clients than ever. So what were we really doing there except hustling after a barely viable idea?

Your Philosophy

That is what will be important for you to decide. What your purpose is. What is your guiding and driving force within you that propels you daily and makes you tick. For me, I was trying to force myself into a system that didn't match my views and how I work.

Perhaps you can relate to stories like this. I'm sure you can, actually. We all have them. Each of us is an individual and it's

2 A SPECIAL CLASS OF PEOPLE

"Having been poor is no shame, being ashamed of it is." – Ben Franklin

I say you're part of a special class of people because there are few people who seem to have the right mix of skills, perseverance, and risk tolerance that successful entrepreneurs do. Most entrepreneurs' businesses fail. Lack of one of those areas may be the reasons why. Some of us are born with higher tolerances than others. And, I don't think it's wrong to say that any of those things can't be learned to put together a well rounded entrepreneur. But, in any case, whether innate or learned, few people will ever possess them.

Most people are not even willing to put hard work in to learn things that will make them successful on all fronts. If you went to any employee, in a specialized job, in any American company today, and told them that it would be in their interest to learn something about what another department in their company does, chances are, they'd tell you that's not their job. The vast majority of people aren't interested in that kind of thing at all.

You, on the other hand, have to wear many hats. You're forced to. And you're forced to wear them well or risk failure. You have to be able to absorb stress of risk and unknown and still sleep at night and get up early for work the next day. You're not only making your own job, you're making them for other people as well. And you have to make sure that everyone gets to eat before you do.

There aren't many of us in the country or even world that are willing to do or even tolerant of that. But, small business is critically important to the American economy. And despite what would seem to be economically depressing events and huge obstacles put in place by the governments, people continue to start businesses and churn out products and services. In some ways, more now than ever before. If this is you, congratulations. Welcome to our club! You're special and part of something vital to the health of our entire nation, if not the world.

3 EMPLOYMENT FALLCIES

"It's the government's fault. It's corporate America's fault. It's (insert your favorite scapegoat's name here) fault." Listen to your friends talk. Perhaps you have been guilty of such thinking.

It's antiquated to think of landing one "secure" job and saving for retirement. We have already established that there is no security. Any feeling of security is only in your head – even if you think you are protected by the law or by being a member of an organization like a union. Anything could happen at any time. The law may say one thing, but there's no guarantee that you'll ever receive a remedy. As long as you are strictly someone's employee at one company, you're a liability on the balance sheet. I say that as a business owner. We cannot trust any government to provide us with what we need, nor is that its responsibility. We cannot trust most employers either. Insulate yourself or by working for yourself.

Opportunities, resources, deals, and money are all around. We must condition ourselves to see the opportunities so we can connect the dots and put together lucrative transactions. Usually. people think money and wealth are scarce. That's partially true. What makes things more valuable? Their scarcity. Jobs are scarce. People are waiting around for companies to benevolently bestow employment upon them. Wealth can take many forms and mean different things to different people. The same is true for the concept of value. What one person finds valuable, another may not. Value, like beauty, is in the mind of the beholder.

People with a scarcity attitude see a lack everywhere; a lack of jobs, lack of money, lack of opportunities. Often, that kind of thinking leads to resentment of other people or groups. They want to take rather than give or create!

People with an attitude of wealth see opportunities and resources everywhere. They see a wealth of deals to be made, relationships to develop, and resources of which to take advantage. They are givers. Their kind of thinking can liberate minds from the confines of an attitude of scarcity. An attitude of wealth doesn't foster resentment of others. It opens doors and possibilities. Try to foster this attitude in yourself.

Thinking in terms of wealth versus scarcity is an attitude that develops with time and practice. After years of being "taught" that we should sacrifice for others, that we should not be selfish, it's hard to break those old thoughts.

Opportunities are limitless. There are always deals to be made. You need to rewire your brain to see them, not wait around for someone else to give you a small piece after the fact. Manage the power!

People often think money comes from:

1. Their boss

2. Rich people

3. The government

It actually comes from *assets and customers*. Unless you realize this, you may be tempted to sit back and wonder why people higher up the corporate ladder or in government aren't giving you more of it. You've done a good job, of course you deserve it. But, will they even notice? You've got to take it from the customers, your own customers, yourself. And you need to buy assets that pay you going forward.

Scarcity can be good in a specialized, hard-to-come-by skill, but as far as money, value, and "wealth" are concerned, there is more than enough to go around. The most valuable commodity in the universe is information and/or the knowledge that comes with learning that information. Do not feel guilty or have hang ups about being successful or propelling yourself forward.

Apart from a good learning attitude the most important assets are the people with whom you keep company.

Remember, you are the sum of the five people with whom you spend the most time!

Imagine that you tell your five beer-drinking poker buddies that you want to venture on your own and make a fortune. What would they tell you? They would laugh their socks off before tearing your ego into a million pieces.

At the heart of man lies jealousy. Some don't want to see the people around them succeed. If you succeed, it makes them look bad. They know in their hearts that they are going nowhere yet they embrace that attitude and pull you down with them. They will steal your dream, and rob you of your financial freedom if you are not careful!

It's the crab mentality. Any one crab could climb up out of the fisherman's bucket and escape, but the others will always grab hold and drag him back to their level. They will self-police to the point that none of them can escape the predicament in which they find themselves.

The key point: mix only with positive minded people. Positive thinking is not wishful thinking. A wishful thinker is a dreamer who doesn't take action. Positive thinking is backed by action. You will feel the energy of people who believe in you and support your dreams.

If you hang out with ducks, you will quack ... but if you hang out with eagles, you will soar!

Fill yourself with positive information. Associate with positive people. Fill your mind with inspiring material. Don't spend time chatting about negatives that bring people down. Get rid of that negative energy. People avoid negativity. Look for people who follow your vision or are willing to grow with you.

Lastly, you must BELIEVE IN YOURSELF! Stepping out of your comfort zone may seem terrifying. Many will not support your dream and go on the offensive. It could be your parents or your spouse.

You may be faced with the question; is my financial freedom worth the price I am paying? Can I live another day with the same routine, the same job, the same pay check or the same drudgery? If the answer is no, then take action NOW, not tomorrow, or you could wake and forget your dream.

Write your desire on a piece of paper and hang on tight every day. Share it with someone positive and take that first step. You won't regret it.

4 HOW MOST PEOPLE LIVE

We've sort of been led to believe over years that we are part of this bee hive, so to speak. We aren't groups of individuals. We are all supposed to be selfless and motivated for the good of the whole. Part of that may be true and part of that may not be. We tend to believe things are benevolently bestowed upon us by large companies or the government. Everything we have, we owe to them and should thank them. Our parents were born into a certain "class" of people and we should remain relatively within that same "class" too.

We've Been Conditioned this Way

It's not all our fault. This is what has been ingrained in us since we were young. We've lost sight of our heritage and what made us a prosperous society to begin with. We've been conditioned this way. I'm not saying it's some vast conspiracy or anything, but we've settled into a place of complacency and comfort as a society, it seems. It's not happy, but it's better than sudden change or the fear of the unknown for most people.

Did you ever hear anybody say "There's no jobs." Or "We don't have a choice." That is someone who views things as I described above. If there are no jobs, how is that big company working down the street. They may not be hiring right now, but they didn't come here because there wasn't a potential to create jobs.

Or maybe the person that thinks they have no choice, but to work for a company that doesn't pay or value them enough. Or provide the right benefits. Or whatever.

There's always a choice. If that company is in existence, that's an indication to you that customers and money are there. If you don't want to work there, it's up to you to get some of those customers and that money for yourself. Nobody is saying you have to cave to their demands.

This is the basis of opportunity. Most people have been conditioned that risk is bad and aren't willing to take it. As a result, they feel limited in their available choices. Then blame starts being thrown around.

The World Owes you Nothing

Let's be honest and get some things straight. An entitlement attitude will get you nowhere. It seems more and more of the American workforce has or is developing this attitude. The sad reality is that the world owes you nothing. Other than your basic rights to life, liberty, and property and the same right to pursue opportunities as anyone else. The sooner we accept that, the better off we will be.

If you want something you'll have to put in the time and hard work to achieve it or earn it, yourself. Even of all the currently rich people in our country, very few of them have had it handed to them. Sure, some have legacy money, but they are the minority. Most are self-made.

The world is only interested in what you can bring to it. People are not selfless. In order for you to be valuable to the world, you have to create value somehow. You success will all depend on what you can bring to the table, not what someone can give to you.

Accumulate Assets, not Stuff

We see this a lot with baby boomers. They probably grew up poor. As they got older and had an astronomical rise in income and wealth as a generation, they started to accumulate stuff and things. They accumulate for a variety of reasons, maybe it's to display wealth, maybe it's comforting to them, maybe it's a symptom of not having much as children. In any case, it turns out to be a lot of junk that they then need a bigger house to store and it costs more to move. It never gets used. Eventually, it's a headache to clean up and organize.

These are things that suck money from you. They aren't things that contribute to wealth or bettering your standing. Instead of all that stuff, imagine if it went to something that was actually beneficial or putting money in your pocket.

Do All You Agree to Do

In small business you don't really have much to go on. Your reputation and your word are two of your most valuable things you can preserve. People don't know your brand and don't care, most likely. There may not be a lot that separates you from others.

It's very simple to be reliable and do what you have agreed to do. That will instill confidence in people and come across well in referrals. Some industries run rampant with unprofessional people. Construction contractors, some financial institutions, some areas of the health care profession.

It is in your interest not to ever be associated with that kind of thing. If you say you will meet someone at X time, meet them there and be a few minutes early. If you say your service will include XYZ, makes sure it does. The phrase under promise, and over deliver rings true here. Preserve your reputation by being reliable, over delivering, and following through on what you say. Other people's time is valuable too. Don't waste their's and you'll be able to position yourself above all the unprofessional people out there.

Why This Makes You Unhappy

In many organizations much of the labor is so far removed from the customer that employees don't care. They can't see the overall vision, process or outcome. They lose the feeling of ownership in what they are doing. Soon, they join the ranks of the "working dead."

Labor then becomes resentful of management and ownership. Ownership resents labor. Quality of service plummets and customers stop patronizing the business. Many of us live in free countries with individual rights and freedoms to do what we want. But businesses are set up like monarchies or some kind of caste system. Naturally, a worker prefers not to have an over-bearing master or to be bossed around. Yet, in a business, that is often exactly what occurs.

A lot of the way things work now go against your natural human tendencies and preferences. As a country, we value freedom and liberty and autonomy. And then we go to work every day in companies that are set up like monarchies. There's something about that that just seems fundamentally wrong to me. If you're applying to be an employee, you're literally applying to be someone else's liability? Why aspire to that?

5 ENTREPRENEURSHIP: IT'S IN YOUR NATURE

"Everyone is selling something."

Everyone wants to make more money. And people, generally, are split into two categories. There are those who bring results after they are promised wealth first and then there are those who bring the results first, and are rewarded afterwards.

Let's explore the two groups in depth. In the first, those who only move their butts after promises of fat paychecks are more like employees, freshmen, or mercenaries. There is no right or wrong with this kind of thinking, but consider this: you are once again trading your precious time for money. Instead of investing your time in an ASSET that generates money, you spend your time working on something that is short term, for limited wealth, and which does not give you income long after you have stopped working.

Consider also that this kind of short term vision will only produce limited or temporary results, at best. Have you ever seen a security guard asleep at work when the boss is not around? Whenever an employee is offered a higher salary, more medical benefits and longer vacations, the heart starts pumping faster. That is evidence of how emotions rule our chase for the dollar.

A higher salary doesn't mean fewer financial problems though. On the contrary, when your income goes up, your commitments, your tax bracket and the time spent at your workplace increases. The greater your salary, the weaker your position. If your boss is paying you a five figure income and calls an emergency meeting, you had better rush to the office, even if you are half asleep!

A good definition of an employee/boss relationship is this: an employee will only do the bare minimum to keep the boss from firing them and a boss will only pay the bare minimum to keep an employee from leaving.

The second group includes many creative people – some entrepreneurs, business leaders, creators, innovators, consultants, proprietors, and inventors who, typically, generate a lot of ideas.

To succeed, those in the second group need to stop working for money. What does this mean? Isn't making money part and parcel of having good financial IQ?

What I mean by 'stop working for money' is not working for free. Work, instead, to gain the necessary skills you need to be a successful entrepreneur (or inventor). To illustrate: if you lack the contacts for running a business, the best place to look for contacts is where? Your competitor's customers, of course.

How about product knowledge? Work with a company that can teach you the skills and the tricks of the trade.

Not familiar with the production line of a factory? Work in one! Learn the ropes, or manage the factory workers.

Fearful of talking to people? Get a sales job where you will be forced to talk all the time. It is also a great way to develop perseverance!

The best education you can get is in real life – not in a lecture hall!

However, remember this: not everybody has what it takes to succeed as an entrepreneur!

Many lack the perseverance, the creative mindset, the financial capabilities or the necessary contacts to get the job done. Some give up too early before any results can be seen! The fastest way to get those skills to succeed is to learn them hands on and get paid in the process! Don't be sidetracked by how much you are paid.

When Donald Trump was selecting candidates in *The Apprentice*, he set their first task: go to the streets and sell lemonade! Many would find it degrading. But to The Donald, it was very important. If you can't do something as simple as sell lemonade, how can you handle a daunting task like running the Trump empire?

Again, let me ask: would you trade time for short term money (money that stops coming in when you stop)?

Or, would you trade time and money for a long term asset that generates income (even long after you have stopped)?

We all have a brain. All we need is to look around and find problems to overcome. Every problem is an opportunity in disguise.

It's up to you. You may or may not see the results in the short term, but by using your brain and available resources, you can create true value for which others are willing to pay.

It is important that when designing this part of your life, you don't take something you love and turn it into something you hate by making it seem like work. Let's take my custom kayak fishing rod revenue stream as an example. If I had to market, prospect, hunt down leads, try to turn them into paying customers, build the rods myself then ship them off, I'd probably hate it. I do market them, but as it turns out, I meet a lot of people who are interested in the same activity. I use my product. It's visible. Others can see it and feel it. The conversation will turn to how they can get one of my rods. I can give them a business card where they can order straight from my website.

Alternatively, I may sell one on the spot. I do not manufacture them myself. I enjoy the design process but I have a someone who procures the parts and assembles them for me under my label. That's the hard part. All I have to do is order them, mark them up 100 per cent on our website, sell them, and ship them off. Interacting with the customers is fun and easy, an activity we all enjoy. It's not a lot of work for me. If I had to do all parts of the process myself, I probably wouldn't do it for very long. So think about how you can take your passions and interests and turn them into a revenue stream that doesn't require a whole day of your time.

6 AMERICAN ENTREPRENEURIAL HISTORY

An entrepreneurial economy is what made America great. People didn't come to settle the country several hundred years ago for all the good paying jobs. There weren't any. There was nothing but natural resources (they thought there was a lot more gold than there was) and opportunities. Many enterprising individuals recognized the opportunities in tobacco. Even the months it took to ship goods and currency thousands of miles across oceans wasn't off-putting. People were merchants. They had skills and performed the requisite services and were also intimately connected to their customers. They could see the direct relationship between the quality of their efforts and the rewards for those efforts.

We went from a struggling group of colonies to the most prosperous nation the world has ever seen in record time. That's an amazing accomplishment. It wasn't all rosy. There have been abuses of power, rights violations, violence, and more. But, luckily, those things were in the minority. By and large, it has been a combination of our relative safety concerning geographic location in the world, our cultural values, and our freedom to pursue our interests. With our two large oceans on each side and two peaceful borders to the North and South, we have been free from fear of invasion or being conquered. We have been free to pursue commerce relatively uninterrupted building wealth along the way. People in tightly packed European countries with hostile neighbors all around could not say the same over the same time period. We value individualism and having a strong work ethic. Combine that with unbridled commerce and you have even more wealth building.

Early in our history we had men like Ben Franklin who ran multiple operations through a variety of skills. Some small ventures and others grew to be rather large. Later there were very shrewd men like Ford, Carnegie, and Rockefeller who dominated their industries. Ford probably being the best at skillfully navigating his relationships with his own labor, his customers, and the government.

America has sat nicely in our corner of the world and lined our pockets over the last couple centuries. There's no telling how things may have turned out had we gone about things better with native populations, our participation in slavery, and our own clashes from within. Regardless, we are where we are today because of or in spite of those things.

Immigrants continue to arrive in America for the freedom to pursue the many opportunities here. Sadly, many Americans have become blind to opportunities. Instead, many play the blame game. Blaming other individuals or groups for their current poor standing. I love to see and speak to people who have come here to pursue these opportunities. It might be the Hispanic man running his landscaping company, the Indian man who's so happy to be here to develop his software, or the Canadian financial advisor. They're all here to work and produce something bigger. Every transaction that takes place produces more wealth.

It's Time to Get Back to that History

Today, we have become spoiled. We expect things for nothing or without proving our worth first. In my opinion, the expectations among employers and employees is almost so far gone it might be impossible to save so that they can reasonably work together.

Maybe it's time more of us recognize those fallacies and start looking to support and do things ourselves. As with the quote above, "Everyone is selling something." You're already doing it if you're an employee. You're currently selling your labor or skills to an employer for as much as you can. They are buying for as little as you'll take. That's the market price for your labor and, make no mistake, you are the proprietor selling it to them. Why not do the same except keep more of the fruits of your labor?

Would it really be that much different? Would it make you less happy? Chances are it would be a little uncomfortable, but I bet it would make you more happy in the long run. It's more in line with our nature and should be more rewarding on a personal level.

7 THE HOW: DECIDING WHAT YOU WANT

Based on what we considered in your overall philosophy above, you'll have some decisions to make. Your business should feed or fund your life. A sure recipe for unhappiness would be to set up a business that clashes with your life's vision. It should be a tool to allow you to do what you want to do. Be sure the vision for your life is fed by the vision of your business.

Three Ways of Making Money

It's quite simple.

1. Trade time for money – employees, self-employed.

2. Manifest and use creative ideas – inventors, artists, programmers, and innovators.

3. Leverage resources and other people – business people, leaders.

If you are a professional, have you explored writing an ebook or creating a course about your field of expertise? If well written, it could provide a new income stream, instead of you selling out your time serving your clients.

How about a computer programmer? You can produce your own revolutionary product or software instead of selling your ideas to the company for which you work.

How about real estate? Instead of selling homes, you could pool financial sources to buy cheap houses, increase their value with inexpensive updates and sell them off at a higher price. It just takes a little time and research to find good ideas.

Is money a problem? Seek loans if you can take the risk. Pool money from investors or seek a grant. The sky is the limit.

Which way do you want to achieve wealth? Answer: it's totally up to you.

A lot of people are opposed to change, even if it's for the better. Many situations persist simply because "it's the way we've always done it" or "this is just how it's done." Consider whether there might be one or multiple other ways to go about your life rather than what "conventional wisdom" dictates. Might there be a way around the status quo? Yes, of course, there is. There are probably infinite ways to go about your life.

I'm lucky. I tend to not follow norms and usually buck trends. Just because "everyone else does it that way" could mean I do something different simply out of spite. Call it what you want; trendsetting, not following the herd, or perhaps a slightly rebellious attitude. I don't want to be a member of the "working dead."

8 STRUGGLE IN THE LEAN TIMES

Without question, you will work very hard and long early on especially if building a business from scratch. Even if buying into something like a franchise where everything is created for you, the initial work set up can be lengthy and time consuming. There is every reason to believe that it will be a long time until the first sale is made. That is, unless you have a ready made network built up ahead of time or demand for a product before it is even out yet.

Many businesses may have a one to five year plan to pay back initial debt financed loans. Sales will be sparse. Cash flow will be inconsistent. And you may not be in the black for over a year.

You'll be exhausted in the building process and probably beyond that. You'll be working nights and weekends. Probably in addition to your current job while you build what you want. This is where it's critically important to manage your energy.

There will be lots of struggles learning hard lessons early on. That's true monetarily speaking and elsewhere in your business.

9 FATIGUE, PERSISTENCE, AND YOUR WILL

Managing Your Time or Your Energy

One of the benefits of entrepreneurship is you can make your own schedule and work when you are most productive. If I sit down and try to work straight through a full work day, I have trouble, particularly if looking at a computer screen for long periods. It's hard on both my eyes, and my brain concentrating on multiple tasks simultaneously. I need periodic breaks so I can maintain focus. Have you noticed that your best ideas come in the shower or while driving in your car, but you can't summon them when sitting at the work computer?

I know my body's rhythms and I am not energetic throughout the entire day. My most productive times are between 6 and 8 am while around 10.30 am is a good time to stop for a quick snack. I have a serious energy and mental acuity crash around 2 to 3 pm. A power nap is not out of the question. Many times, I'll keep my laptop with me on the couch after dinner while I watch TV for several hours between about 7 and 11 pm. This is a good time to connect with friends and others on social media. At the same time I have good ideas reading other material and may get a burst of productivity then too. If nothing else, I have ideas for the next day. My productivity isn't in one giant, solid block of time. Likely, yours isn't either. Recognize that and make the most of your best times.

Health and Fitness for Entrepreneurs

Running a business is hard enough as it is, but many people make it even harder on themselves. Your personal health can have a BIG impact on the health of your business too, so make sure you keep it a priority. There is a price for being an entrepreneur. Sometimes even a high psychological price. It's in your and your business' interest to mitigate as much of that risk as you can.

To start with, here are 10 unhealthy personal health habits that could hurt your business. Keep these in mind and look for their warning signs.

Getting Angry

There's simply no way that getting angry helps you in business. When you get angry, your emotion overwhelms and blinds you. It also adds stress to what's already a stressful lifestyle. Learn to control your anger and always make decisions from a place of calm and reason.

Self-Doubt

It's only natural that when you start a business, you'll have your fair share of self-doubt. But too much self-doubt can keep you from taking actions that need to be taken to grow your business. When doubt raises its ugly head, remember that every business owner was inexperienced and unsure of themselves when they started out. No one is born a business owner knowing exactly what to do at any given time. Many of us are making the best decisions we can, given the limited information we have at any one time.

Thinking You Know What You Don't

One of the worst things for a business owner to say is, "I know that already." For example, it's dangerous to make assumptions about your target market based on what you think they like. You need objective data about your market on which to base your decisions. Evidence. If you're too set in your own opinions, you may be ignoring important new information that comes along. Keep your mind open and be open to knowing what you don't currently really know.

Bad Stress Management

When you start a business, it's important to look at how you deal with stress and decide whether you deal with it in a healthy way or not. There will be more stress ahead in the journey of running your own business. If you don't handle stress well, now is the time to learn some new coping strategies.

Working Until You Burn out

There are countless things to do and only so many hours in a day. This is why so many small business owners push themselves to work long hours, neglecting sleep and leisure activities. This leads to burnout, which can seriously damage your business. Decide on a work schedule and stick to it. Avoid working longer hours unless it's absolutely necessary. Make no mistake, the further you push yourself into fatigue, the longer it takes to recover to productivity again.

Failure to Delegate

New business owners often think they have to do everything themselves. Running a business on the internet, you can do most things yourself. But this doesn't mean that you *should*. Instead of trying to do everything yourself, learn to ask for help when you need it and delegate tasks that drain your time or that are better left in someone else's hands.

Fear of Spending Money

Business owners need to consider cash flow and cut costs where they can, but you shouldn't always look for the lowest price. There are some things that you simply have to pay for. Some business owners shoot themselves in the foot by choosing low price over quality.

Not Listening

Listening is one of the best skills you can have as a business owner. Whether it's a colleague, customer or co-worker that's talking, don't tune them out. In order to make your business a success, you have to meet the expectations of others, and you can't do this unless you listen to them.

Multitasking

People think they're being productive when they multi-task but usually it's the exact opposite. When you perform multiple tasks at the same time, it's hard to give any of them the attention they require. Focus on one task at a time.

Fear in General

It's natural and healthy to feel fear and acknowledge it. But it can stop you from taking action. True courage means taking action in spite of the fear you feel. Push the fear aside and get down to business.

Running your own business is challenging but also deeply rewarding. Do your best to recognize and cut out unhealthy habits and replace them with habits that help you to succeed.

Manage Your Health Under Pressure

Few people realize just how stressful it is to start your own business. While you're free of bosses, strict scheduling, and the other pressures of a regular job, you'll find new stresses that come from working for yourself. Here are ten things you can do to help you combat the stress of starting your own business.

Meditation

One thing that many entrepreneurs share is a love of meditation. Studies show that meditation activates parts of your brain associated with stress relief. It allows you to reach a relaxed state where your mind can wander so that you can be more productive when you need focus. Work a short meditation session into your day. It doesn't have to take the classic form of what we imagine meditation to be. It can be anything that allows you to re-center yourself and not have your mind racing for a few minutes or hours. For me, sitting quietly fishing allows me to do that by focusing only on the activity at hand that is pleasing and soothing to me.

Deep Breathing

Deep breathing is even simpler than meditation but it can achieve the same effect. It involves sitting somewhere comfortable and taking in deep breaths. It can be combined with aromatherapy, music or meditation. The more oxygen you bring into your body, the less tension you feel.

Socialize

Take some time each day to meet someone face to face and socialize. Make a lunch date or an afternoon coffee break out of it. The act of simply meeting a friend offers great stress relief. You can vent about your stresses and get them off your chest, or escape the day by discussing something totally unrelated.

Take a Mental Vacation

Picture a relaxing place and imagine that you're there. You can get a picture of this place to gaze at, or just picture it in your mind. It could be a sunny beach, a quite mountainside or anywhere else you feel calm. Try to imagine this place with all five of your senses. If not only in your mind, maybe it's a change of scenery locally for you. Maybe you choose to work in the quiet coffee shop with the white noise background down the street when you usually work at home.

Get Active

Activity is one of the greatest stress reducers. It doesn't have to be anything strenuous at all. Try stretching, doing some simple exercises like push-ups, or going for a long walk. Anything that gets your heart pumping releases endorphins in your brain that help you naturally cope with stress.

Eat

Eating can help you relieve stress. Asparagus, avocado, blueberries, almonds, oranges, salmon, spinach, turkey and a whole host of other foods contain natural ingredients that help you stay on an even keel. Eat as much fresh, natural food as possible and avoid food that is overly processed or high in sugar.

Natural Stress Relievers

Natural stress relievers can be things as simple as sitting quietly and drinking herbal tea. Or petting your cat for a few minutes.

Sleep More and Better

Sleep is probably the best stress reliever and all you need to do is to close your eyes. Lack of sleep prevents your brain from functioning properly and you'll find yourself getting stressed over little things. Don't convince yourself that because of your busy schedule, it's okay to skimp on sleep.

Ask for Help

You don't have to do everything yourself when you run your own business. Enlist others to help you, outsource whatever tasks you can, and look into automating your business processes.

Get Rid of Stressors

If you feel stressed, take a minute to figure out exactly what causes your stress. Is there any way you can eliminate it? For example, a certain client may be particularly stress-inducing. Changing up your work schedule may help. See if there is any way to get rid of any of your stressors.

Finally, it's good to realize that not all stress is bad. Sometimes it's good to feel like you're under the gun. It gives you a good kick in the rear to get you moving. But when you're overwhelmed by stress, you need to combat it.

10 Tips on Balancing Work and Life for Entrepreneurs

One of the biggest challenges you face when starting a business is your work/life balance. You find yourself working around the clock and neglecting all other areas of your life. It's a tough struggle because it takes so much work to get a business off the ground. It's easy to convince yourself to give up your day off or lunch break in order to get essential things done.

However, if you don't properly maintain a good work-life balance, it can destroy your health, personal relationships and sanity. Here are ten tips for keeping this important balance. But, let's be clear, this may not be balance in the same sense most people, or even you, were thinking about it. You certainly cannot do it all or have it all. That's a reality. And you need to do what you need to do to satisfy your home life, whatever that looks like. But, you wouldn't be able to support your home life, or maybe family, if it wasn't for your work life. It may not be an even split in time devoted to each area. That's not what I'm talking about here. Early on, your family might forget your name or what you look like. If that's what you have to do and you can still satisfy what you need to do at home, then that's just the way it is.

Establish Clear Start and Stop Times

When you start working for yourself, you're always on the clock. It's important to establish a clear starting and stopping time for your workday. Otherwise, work can spill over into your mornings, evenings and weekends. That's the sacrifice many people make early on. What can help is ending your work day in a good spot. Some logical stopping point. There will always be more work. But, don't leave something unresolved and then try to go home and talk to family or go to sleep. Your mind will just continue to race and you won't be present. On the opposite side of a logical stopping point, give yourself a few daily tasks in a bulleted list that you must get done the next day. That way you know exactly what you have to do and don't spend the first couple hours getting in the right frame of mind or putting out fires.

Schedule Downtime

If work is keeping you from doing other things, put these other things on your schedule right alongside work tasks. Plan your leisure activities, even if they're watching TV or playing with the kids. If you have a busy schedule and don't plan these activities, they may not happen.

When Off, Be Really Off

During your non-work time, disconnect from email, Skype or other communications. If there is something you feel you need to deal with, tell yourself you'll do it first thing in the morning or first thing Monday. Be sure to relay that to any business associates who may be waiting on communication from you. This is true especially if you have to be focused and present on family or someone else's needs at the moment. But, let's not lose sight of the fact that this is who we are, this is how we identify ourselves. This is what should excite you. There have already been many parts of this book written at two or three am simply because I was on a roll, excited, and sleep was the furthest thing from my mind. Currently, it is 11:58pm on a SATURDAY night and I'm here hammering away because, although I could really be "off", I feel good and I'm willing to work when other people aren't.

Set Aside a Day or Two

When starting a new business, it's easy to work seven days a week, especially when these aren't full days of work. But it's a good idea to have at least one day completely free of work, from when you wake up to when you go to sleep. Set aside this day and make it a goal to set aside a second day. Ultimately, we are working towards more freedom as entrepreneurs. But, that may be down the road. Again, in the beginning, you do what you have to do, especially if that means while working another job while you build something else. Nights and weekends may be your only options.

Be Accountable

It's hard to keep work and life separate by yourself. Tell your family, friends or colleagues about your times and days off. Promise family members you'll spend time with them. Ask them to hold you accountable and it's much easier to stick to your schedule. Do what you have agreed to do just as you would in any other business agreement. Don't cancel.

Outsource and Automate

One great way to maintain the balance is to get rid of some of the things you have to do. Take advantage of outsourcing and automation to get some tasks off of your to-do list. Now we're really moving toward that freedom for you.

Start an Idea File

Create an idea file or other system for when inspiration strikes during your time off. Your smart phone likely has a thousand apps for this. When you get an idea or suddenly remember something you need to do, write it down and file it away for your next working shift. For example, email any ideas you get to your work email and they'll be waiting for you when you next start work.

Upgrade Your Organizing

If you get better organized, you'll increase your productivity and gain better control over your work day. If you're disorganized and scattered, you'll feel like you always have endless things to do. Create a daily work flow where the highest priority items come first. If at the end of the day you're left with low-priority items only, it's much easier to call the day over and do them tomorrow if need be.

Get in Touch with Your Rhythms

Everyone has their own natural rhythms when it comes to work and productivity. Try to discover your rhythms and set your schedule accordingly. For example, if you find that you have high energy during the mornings and evenings but you're dragging through the afternoons, work a split shift where you have the afternoon off to enjoy leisure activities. Remember, manage your energy, maybe not your time. To be successful, you must persist long after others would have given up. You must pace yourself. Don't drive yourself into the ground. Perseverance and your will to go on will set you apart.

Know What You Can and Can't Control

There's only so much you can control your work-life balance. Sometimes (or often, it may seem), unexpected things happen. If life interrupts your workday, take the day off and deal with it. If there's a real work-related emergency on a day off, let yourself take care of it.

If you watch your work-life balance and learn some good strategies for keeping them in check, you'll find yourself increasingly getting a handle on it. After a while, you'll find more time outside of work. But still, it's a good thing to think about from time to time and make changes if necessary.

Tips for Avoiding the "Freshman 15" of Start Ups

The term "freshman 15" refers to the weight many students put on during their first semester of college. When you start college, you settle into a less active, more sedentary lifestyle. Add dorm food and beer to the mix and you have a recipe for disastrous weight gain.

The same thing happens when you first start a business. You now spend your day hunched over a laptop, wolfing down meals between tasks, and sleeping whenever you have free time.

"Computer butt," as the start-up version of the freshman 15 is jokingly called, occurs for two reasons – lack of exercise and poor diet. Sleep habits and stress also play a part. Overall, there are four steps you need to take to ensure your health and fitness.

Know your metabolism. Know how many calories you need to maintain, gain, or lose fat. Eating less will cause a loss, more will cause a gain. Get in the habit of looking at your calorie intake just like you would any other budget.

Eat some of each of the food stuffs at each meal and snack. This will prevent hormone surges or drops and slow digestion. A mix of protein, carbohydrates, and fats, in proportions that are suitable to your lifestyle, are what you want to aim for.

Eat a variety. You'll get a wider range of nutrients and help to avoid deficiencies as well as break up boredom of the same foods over and over.

Exercise and play. Don't confuse the two. Play is recreation or simple activity just for the sake of or enjoyment of it. You want to engage in this as much as possible as long as it isn't harmful. Exercise is a planned and structured process. You'll want to exercise the all of the major muscle groups of the body 2 or 3 times per week, on non-consecutive days, in a progressive manner, with conventional exercises. Circuit weight training with appropriate and challenging resistances is a great way to include a cardiovascular/endurance component at the same time you are working your muscular system. It will save you time and be safe and effective. Workouts should last approximately 30 minutes.

Here are additional things you can do to combat that dreaded weight gain and keep yourself healthy as you get your business off the ground.

Observe Meal Times

Take the time you need to cook and eat well. When you first start working for yourself, meals are rushed. You reach for the nearest processed food that you can zap in the microwave. But you need to make time for meals. Meal-time gives you a much needed break. It gives you not only rest but also the fuel you need. Make the effort to keep eating well.

Go for Variety

Planning and thinking about meals seems like a drain on your time when you work for yourself. But part of eating healthy is eating a variety. Make sure you're getting many different nutrients and not only eating the same few things.

Watch the Snacking

When you have long hours in front of the computer, you're likely to treat yourself to a snack, especially when working at night. When you get a snack attack, reach for something healthy. Avoid the junk food trap. Keep your house stocked with healthy snacks that you can eat easily for when cravings hit.

Drink Plenty of Water

When you need something to eat or drink, pour yourself a glass of water. Water helps you maintain your concentration. It offers a healthy drink that's not sugar-filled like soda. Another nice thing about water is that it can make you feel full, which helps to prevent overeating.

Don't Skip Meals

When you're busy getting your business off the ground, it's tempting to skip meals, especially breakfast. But this is not a healthy lifestyle choice. Skipping meals can throw your metabolism out of whack and cause stress. Eat a balanced breakfast and make sure you're eating lunch and dinner as well.

Walk Whenever You Can

Take the opportunity to walk rather than drive every chance you get. If you usually drive to a store that's just a 20-minute walk away, walk it. If you take the train two short stations, walk the distance instead. Bring along some music or podcasts to get your mind off of work.

Sleep Much and Often

It's only natural that when you get busy, sleep seems like a luxury rather than a necessity. But you need that time unconscious to balance your stress level and give your brain what it needs to get the work done. Make sure that you get enough sleep and try to keep a regular sleeping schedule.

Watch Your Weight

Even if you've always been fit and never worried about weight gain, start thinking about it now. You'll be surprised at the pounds you put on, even if it's never been an issue before. Controlling your calories is no different than any other budget. It takes some practice, but you can get it down to a skill and be able to manage things appropriately should you find yourself creeping up.

You may not have the most strenuous day job in the world, but when you switch to the sedentary lifestyle of an entrepreneur starting up their business, you're bound to put on some pounds. Use these ten tips to keep computer butt at bay.

Tips for Achieving a Healthy Mindset for Business Success

It takes more than technology, skills, or experience to achieve success in business. You also need to have the proper mindset. Here are 10 tips for fostering the healthy mindset that will help you attain your business goals.

Your Offering to the World

Obviously your business exists in order to make a profit. That's how a business keeps running. But rather than thinking about money, growth or success, frame it differently. Consider how your business is going to help people. What are you going to offer to the world? This is a better mindset because it allows you to put your customers first and meet their needs.

State Your Vision

Clearly identify exactly what it is you'd like to do with your business. Without a clear image or purpose, it's impossible for you to attain your business goals. Successful people spend a great deal of time thinking about purpose and vision. Create a vision for your business and write it down. Keep this vision handy when you need inspiration or direction.

Don't Fear Rejection

There's always a fair amount of selling, whether you're making cold calls directly or simply putting your offer out there online. Selling is uncomfortable for people because of the fear of rejection. If a customer rejects your offer, it feels like they're rejecting you personally. Learn to recognize that it's the offer or product and not you that is being rejected.

Turn Failures into Lessons

Successful people learn by making mistakes and failing. Through these failures they learn how to run their business and gain valuable experience. Learn to see your mistakes as important lessons and learn everything you can from them.

Think about Growth

People typically consider things fixed. They believe they have fixed abilities, fixed talents, fixed character traits, and so on. Instead of a fixed mindset, try to cultivate a growth mindset, where you consider future potentials rather than accepting things as they are.

Running a Business Is a Journey

Learn to love the journey and process, and not just the end result. Running a business is a journey. There's no shortcut or easy way to realize your dreams. It's an adventure full of daily surprises where you gradually see your goals coming to fruition.

Take Responsibility

When things go wrong, it's easy and comforting to blame others. Others may actually be the ones to blame. But if you take responsibility for whatever happens in your business, this puts you in a position of power where you can direct and change things. Whenever something goes wrong, even if it wasn't your fault, try to understand what you could've done differently and learn from it.

Value Your Time

Successful people are excellent time managers. Plan your working time in order to get the most out of it. Avoid activities that waste time or don't use it effectively. Time management is a skill that takes time to learn, so try different techniques to see what works, and monitor results.

Stop Self-Sabotaging

Try to identify ways you may be sabotaging yourself so that you can get to the root of the problem. Things like procrastination and perfectionism are often manifestations of inner fears or other problems.

Learn to Love Change

There's only one constant when you run a business and that's change. Some business owners fear change and perceive it as a threat to their business. Others embrace it with all of its new opportunities and potential gains. When change comes along, get excited about meeting it.

All of the above tips involve creating new habits of thinking, which can take some time. But the effort you put in to creating this healthy mindset will pay you back for years to come.

10 GETTING ORGANIZED

"If you fail to plan, you are planning to fail!" – Benjamin Franklin

To help you keep things straight, click here to download a zip file with categorized folders http://goo.gl/rVRWod in which to store your business documents and tools. Back these systems up in a safe place, preferably online, so you won't lose your business processes should something happen to your computer. Be extra careful with any sensitive data like client credit card numbers and make sure they are in a secure place.

Writing a business plan is a big task. Many people end up forgoing it altogether. That is a mistake. Thankfully, it need not be a massive document to be effective. It can be scribbled on a piece of scrap paper as long as it offers some direction and considerations.

In order to get funding from a bank or an investor or something, you will probably need a full-fledged plan. You many even want to have someone else like an accountant or attorney help you in the preparation. But, you can accomplish a lot with a business plan worksheet. In fact, it might even be more effective than a big long document you spend a lot of time preparing because things change in business. You will want to revisit your plan periodically. At least annually if not semi-annually.

Being able to quickly work through a worksheet and update as needed can be an added bonus to doing business efficiently and staying agile as changes come your way.

Start by filling in the worksheet below by answering the questions to the best of your ability in as much detail as possible. Should you need a full plan, you can take each section of this worksheet and extrapolate it out into individual sections of a plan.

Business Plan Worksheet

What is your business model(s)?

Description of business (Executive Summary consider writing last):

Vision?

Mission?

Who is your target market(s)?
(summary from Marketing Plan)

Your Unique Selling Proposition

- What are you offering?

- What problem does it solve?

- What is different about you?

- What are your revenue channels?

- Who is your competition?

- Why should people buy from you vs. the competition?

Business Goals
(summary from goal setting worksheet)

- Long Term Goals

- Short Term Goals

- Who is your management team?

SWOT Analysis

- What are you top strengths?

- What are your top weaknesses?

- What are your key opportunities for success?

- What are the threats to your business?

Business Growth and Exit Strategies

- What is your growth strategy?

- What is your exit strategy?

Business Profitability:
(combine all projects plus general business expenses and other revenue)

Total Estimated Expenses (total expenses for all projects combined and general business expenses)	

Total Estimated Revenue (total revenue for all projects combined)	
Total Estimated Profit (total revenue – total profit)	
Estimated Return on Investment (total profit/total expense)	
Estimated Growth Annual	
Estimated 3-5 Year Growth	

Note: If not including your time in expenses, estimate the value of your time per project by calculating:

Total Profit for Project:
Total Hours Spent:
Hourly Profit:

Organizational Chart and Accountability
Your organization should have an organizational chart if you have more than one person working within it. Even if it is just you, it may help to organize the roles in which you'll play and the associated responsibilities that are necessary for each role. You can fill in the most important responsibilities in each box for each position for accountability purposes.

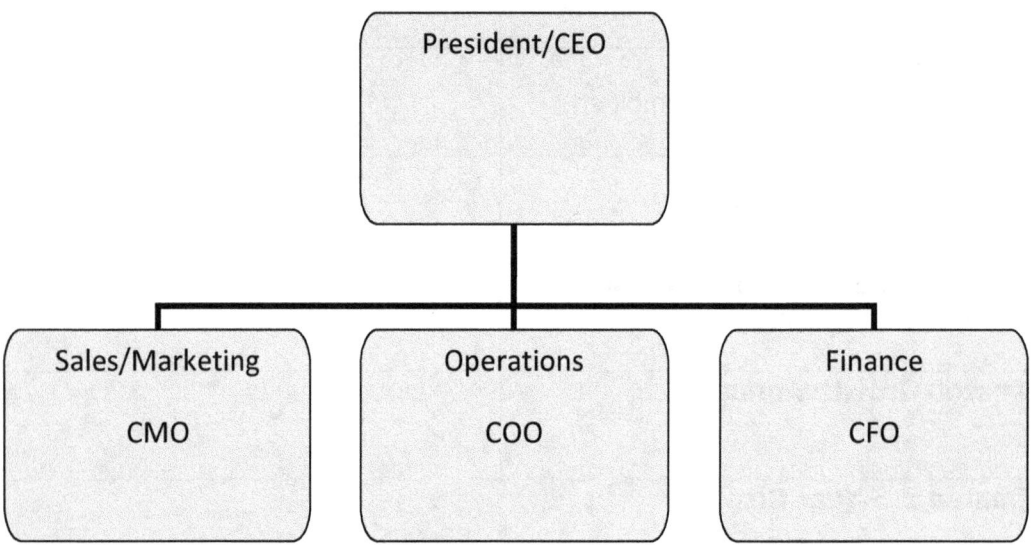

Business Performance Tracker Checklist

For each question, answer Yes or No

Statement/Question	Answer	Solutions/Resources
You have the interest and drive to start a business in this field.		
You have a good mix of technical skills and business sense.		
You have researched your local market and determined that you have a viable idea or opportunity differentiated from the competition.		
You have a plan in place covering the short term and long term vision.		
You have a clear model and		

clearly defined audience or niche in which to serve.		
You have incorporated your business or are operating as a sole proprietor.		
You have the appropriate classification of who is an employee or contractor.		
You have an accurate and reliable bookkeeping and accounting system in place.		
You can know the state of your business finances at any time.		
Your business has a cash cushion.		
You have budgets set up.		
You keep track of your business expenses.		
You understand how you and your business is taxed. You have access to legal services.		
You are properly insured and/or bonded.		
Your personal finances are in line for when you take money out of your business.		
Everyone in your organization has a clear role and responsibilities in writing.		
You have a clearly established sales system.		
You diversify with other revenue streams.		

You have a marketing plan with an established schedule and systems.		
You have good retention of clients and receive a good amount of regular referrals.		
You have clear and visible written policies in place that you and clients abide by.		
You have a set operating methodology in place that is reproducible by anyone.		
You have a set hiring process, in line with your core values to find the right people.		
You have a set staff training procedure and regular meetings in place.		

If you answered No to any of the above questions, place a task in your to do list that works toward resolving this issue until you have a reliable system in place.

11 SALES AND MARKETING

Sales

The sales process is what occurs immediately at the time when you sit down to present your pricing options and ask them to sign up. Really what sales boils down to is playing up the positives of what you can offer and downplaying any possible negatives. That's it. If it's something you are passionate about, that should be no problem at all.

Marketing drives sales to eventually occur. Although the actual sale can offer an additional marketing opportunity in the form of upsells or an opportunity to get a referral, etc. There are libraries full of sales books you could read to enhance your skill in a sales situation. Not that there is some list of tricks you have to memorize and employ, but that you have to realize the psychology of what is actually happening in that moment. The potential client is not making a rational decision. Ultimately, it may turn out to be in the end, but what is really happening is the prospective client is making an emotional decision. Even if you use logic to appeal to someone's emotion, it will still be an emotion driven decision on their part. It will be in your interest to recognize that and position your message and pitch to appeal to certain aspects that can encourage their decision.

Knowing that this is a psychological process, it will help to know things like the reaction certain words you use to describe or pitch your service can have. For example, certain terminology like the words buy, price, or contract have been shown to hinder or kill the sales process. Either consciously or subconsciously, things like saying the word price may trigger in the person's head that there might be a better price elsewhere that they need to shop around for. You may want to use an alternative word like investment if you can use it in a non-cheesy way. Or, instead of contract, refer to the agreement. Avoid the terms that trigger a negative gut reaction.

In a service environment, whether you are working in your location or on site, you're likely to have a standard place for performing your consultations or first meetings with clients or customers. If possible, I prefer not to sit across a table or desk from a prospective client and try to make a sale. If that is the way it is set up, it is ok. No need to make it more unnatural. But, if possible sit on the same side as the person or sit 90 degrees to them with either you or them at the end of a rectangular table or desk. This just simply removes a barrier between you when you are trying to make a connection. And, you want to work with the person to come to this decision, not in opposition to them like a foe across the table who they have to defeat in a battle of wills. This arrangement works well especially if you are the salesman and you have another employee there to provide the actual service because that's who they will be working with. The employee can wait on the other side of the table while listening in on gathering information from the prospect. When it comes time to ask for the sale, you're next to the prospective client and you're "on their side", both literally, and figuratively.

Sales-How to Set Up ARB in Business

Sales. Everybody thinks it's a dirty word. Many people don't like to do it. Many people falsely believe that it's a bag of tricks you're trying to memorize and pull out on a prospective client. It's not that at all. If you have a thoughtful, thorough, and reasoned consultation process, you've done most of the work already. Sales, in essence, can really boil down to playing up the positives of your service to meet and match the wants/needs of the consumer right at the point of sale. It isn't marketing. Marketing leads to sales. Sales happen right when a transaction is taking place. So, if all has gone according to plan, by the time a prospective client sits down in front of you, there's a better chance than not that they will become a client. In some cases, a much better chance. Most of the hard leg work has been done. You can be confident in this moment. From here on out, we will be talking about what we feel is the best way to charge for your services for all parties involved.

A better way to bill and retain your clients and avoid "selling".

It's no secret; most people hate to sell. They hate to sell themselves and they hate to sell their services. That's fine, a lot of people have a hard time pricing themselves and that gets better with more experience as an entrepreneur. But, if you hate doing it, don't put yourself in a position where you are forced to do it over and over again. What am I talking about?

ARB, or as my bank calls it, automatic recurring billing (ARB). I am fortunate to be in an industry where typically, services are paid for ahead of time. That's great. Different industries may be different, but if you have the opportunity to implement this, you should. You don't have to bill your clients after the fact and constantly chase down up to 50% of them to get paid checks for what you have already performed. So, we are a step ahead on that one.

Now why do most entrepreneurs continue to sell finite services? What happens at the end? You are probably in a position where most of the value of your clients comes from repeat business. Selling a fixed service implies that they will stop at some point. That's not what you want!! You want them to fall in love with you and not be able to exist without you.

Every time you come to an end of a contract or package or whatever you currently sell, you have to resell them again. If they bought a big one up front, how are you going to convince them to buy a big one again? If they see that big dollar amount, they may want to go for the smaller package this time. How are you going to top your original sales pitch to get them to sign up the first time? Worst of all, they may just take it as an opportunity to "take a break" or stop altogether. Does this sound familiar? Wouldn't it be better if you could have a better chance at retaining these people, more predictable and reliable income, and not have to resell people every time they complete their package with you? The fact is, there is.

Just take a look at what your gym does to you. They sign you up with an advance (initiation fee), slowly dribble a recurring monthly fee out of your account...automatically. If they are smart, they locked you into a long term deal like a year or more. Some places will lock you in for 3 years. Those days may be gone for a while though. I like to advertise, and use as a selling point, month to month agreements, but that's because I know the likelihood of someone quitting after only the first month or two is very low. It makes them feel comfortable not having to "commit" to something too big or for too long. The point is that the system is automatic, just like a gym membership. Think of what you are selling as a service membership. Here's how we have done it.

You'll need a business bank account with your EIN number. You can obtain that from the IRS after you are a legal business entity. Once you have your business bank account, ask about their merchant services and the ability to take credit cards. My bank uses a virtual terminal through authorize.net. Even other services like Paypal now have a business account and virtual terminal option with subscription or recurring billing options to make things easy. The point is to find a payment processor that will allow you to take and process credit cards automatically. There will likely be a very small transaction fee and something like 2-3% of the total transaction. And possibly the more volume of transactions you do, the lower your rate will be. It can look like a lot when your statement comes, especially for American Express cards, but with a high priced service, you should be able to maintain relatively high margins to allow for this. Plus, NOT having the headaches of chasing people down, getting bad checks, etc. makes up for the relatively small costs of processing credit cards and doing it automatically.

The crucial feature of this system is the ability to set up recurring payments on a monthly basis automatically. So for every new client I see, I sell them on one of our pricing options. From here on out, it is just a monthly membership. You can choose to charge them an initiation or set up fee if you like if there is some initial work you have to do to get things going. Or not at all. If not, make sure you note that to them so they know how much they are saving. You enter that client's payment amount into your system open ended with no end date and let it roll until they need to stop, if they need to. I've had clients for the better part of a decade on this system and I've never stopped it. Many service oriented businesses can operate this way.

Some programs will let you skip a month or stop the subscription and restart it later. It's very easy to do without having to keep asking them to write big checks or give you their credit card over and over again. The more they feel like they are repeatedly paying you, the more they may consider cutting it out eventually. You want to remove that emotional action from your dealings with them so they see the transaction later on their credit card statement and it's just another bill coming from someone else, not you!!

In the long run, you are more likely to realize the true lifetime value of the client by increasing your retention or stimulating repeat business by charging monthly fees.

For added stability and predictability, pro-rate your client's first month and start their next month on either the 1st or the 15th of the month, whichever is closest to their sign up date. This way you won't have unpredictability by having nothing coming in for eight or 10 days and then $10,000 in one day. It will even out your cash flow and you should know exactly what is coming in twice per month. It will help with your cash flow to pay your own bills. And it should help you with your projections based on your monthly goal of new clients to acquire. Simply add the number of new clients and the resulting revenue to the monthly totals to find what you need to reach your monthly goals. It is a little utilized system, but the best in terms of what we have seen to sell and retain the clients that you worked hard to get.

Marketing

There is a lot of confusion when it comes to marketing. Many people almost regard it as some kind of trickery or mind control. It isn't. It is simply communicating the value of your product or service to consumers in the marketplace. Essentially, letting your potential customers know what you're offering and why or how it can benefit them.

What is isn't is lying or being untruthful. It isn't falsifying or overstating the benefits of what you offer. That's wrong, that can be fraud. Big companies do get in trouble from time to time for making claims that cannot be backed up or validated. For our purposes here, marketing is simply a way for you to let the benefits of your service be known to your prospective clients and to hopefully invoke an emotional response in them pushing them toward your business.

Of course, some things work better than others. Some things you never want to do. There will be some elements of individualism regarding your specific business and who you are targeting specifically, but there can be a science to it. There is lots of research and text books written on marketing principles and consumer behavior. I have many friends who are interested in the science of exercise, but when it comes to marketing, it's as if it's some kind of nebulous spiritual concept. Marketing can be treated in the same way with evidence based proven practices and constant observation of results and tweaking for future effectiveness.

According to Wikiversity, "Marketing refers to channeling the gap between service and product providers to service and product seekers.also known as a way of satisfying needs.

The **marketing mix** or the "4 P's" are:

- Product
- Place
- Promotion
- Price"

The traditional 4 P's could be extended to include 7 P's

- "Product
- Price
- Place
- Promotion
- People
- Positioning
- Packaging

These are employed to satisfy a *target market'* or target demographic (the pool of potential customers).

Example:

- Product: Procter and Gamble introduces a new toothpaste designed to taste good and fight cavities. Logo and packaging designed in bright colors to appeal to kids of elementary school age to encourage more tooth brushing.
- Price: $2.00, and discounted by means of coupons
- Promotion: television and radio commercials, magazine and newspaper ads, and a website; these use bright colors and happy music, perhaps an animated cartoon character for a fun and family-friendly attitude
- Place (or distribution): Supermarkets, drugstores, discount stores such as Wal-Mart

Target demographic:

- Mothers with kids who make toothpaste buying decisions for the family (advertising could be shown on children's programming, prompting kids to ask parents to buy the toothpaste)

Creating Utility

The American Heritage Dictionary defines utility as "the quality or condition of being useful". Utility is further defined as any quality and/or status that provides a product with the capability to satisfy the consumer's wants and needs. Marketing is responsible for creating most of a product's inherent utility.
There are four basic types of utility:

- **Form utility:** production of the good or service, driven by the marketing function. For example, Procter and Gamble turns raw ingredients and chemicals into toothpaste.

- **Place utility:** making the product available where customers will buy the product. Procter and Gamble secures shelf space for the toothpaste at a wide variety of retailers including supermarkets and drugstores.

- **Time utility:** making the product available when customers want to buy the product. The U.S. drugstore chain Walgreens has many locations open 24 hours a day, and since the 1990's has placed most of their newer stores at major intersections.

- **Possession utility:** once you have purchased the product, you have rights to use the product as intended, or (in theory) for any use you would like.

A fifth type of utility is often defined along with the above four types:

- **Image utility:** the satisfaction acquired from the emotional or psychological meaning attached to products. Some people pay more for a toothpaste perceived to be more effective at fighting cavities and whitening teeth."

Begin to think about your personal training business in these terms except with regard to a service rather than a product like toothpaste.

Reference: http://en.wikiversity.org/wiki/Principles_of_marketing

Let's take a look at some of the parts of what will become your marketing plan.

Marketing Plan

Marketing Plan
(complete one for each project, if you have more than one)

Project 1:

Target Market Description: (size, demographics, buying characteristics, problems, etc)	
Marketing Strategy 1:	Key tasks: • • • •
Marketing Strategy 2:	Key tasks:

	•
	•
Marketing Strategy 3:	Key tasks: • •
Marketing Strategy 4:	Key tasks: • •
Marketing Strategy 5:	Key tasks: • •
Marketing Strategy 6:	Key tasks: • •
Marketing Strategy 7:	Key tasks: • •

Action Plan

Initial Project Set Up Tasks	**Deadline**	**Responsibility**

Ongoing Tasks – Per Project	**Deadline**	**Responsibility**

Ongoing Business Tasks (overall business)	Deadline	Responsibility

Potential Obstacles

Obstacle	Resource/Solution	Where to Find It

Other Notes:

Profitability Analysis
(do estimates on separate spreadsheet, per month and year)

Project Profitability:
(complete for each project)

Total Estimated Expenses (total expenses for individual project)	
Total Estimated Revenue (total revenue for individual project)	
Total Estimated Profit	

(total revenue – total profit)	
Estimated Return on Investment (total profit/total expense)	

Networking

Joining the local chamber of commerce, some say it's worth it, some say it's not. I live in the richest county in the nation, Loudoun County, VA. So our chamber is large. Naturally, the people that see you often at the events will just assume you are the authority in the area. That may be because most people don't like to get out and do a lot of networking face to face, but it is crucial that you move out of your comfort zone if you hope to meet new people and drum up new prospects. Once you get the hang of it, these activities are actually quite fun. I've been a member for over 5 years of our's. There are other organizations besides local chambers that specialize in professional networking like Business Networking International (BNI) among others. It's been a good experience, but you need to have a strategy in order to be successful.

Generally, I try to go to as many events as I can. You'll have to make a choice as they do have costs associated with them. So going to a lot can really add up, but could be more than worth it too. For me, if I get 1 or 2 clients a year from chamber activities, it's worth it. Obviously, I'm shooting for more than that. The large breakfasts and after hours mixers are fun and fairly productive. Leadshare is the most productive for us. It's a name for a program which consists of smaller, but closer groups where members join to "share leads". You get exclusivity in the group as you'll be the only business representative in your field. You meet twice a month for lunch or breakfast. Each member gets 30 seconds to stand and introduce themselves and give their elevator speech. You'll want to have a standard and scripted elevator speech and not just wing it. You'll sound a lot more professional and get the vital information out that you need to your fellow group members.

If you don't have an elevator speech, go to www.15SecondPitch.com and it is a tool that will help you craft an effective one. I met my certified financial planner (no commission financial advisor) who is a member of my leadshare group. That was a good connection for me as he is one of only 300 or so fee only advisors in the country. We also work on several joint ventures together. If you have a newsletter, it is a good idea to get the people that you have met and have a good relationship with on the newsletter. Another way you can always stay front of mind with your business associates, partners, and prospects.

Your most successful conversions to clients will be qualified leads. In other words, if you run across someone who needs to sell a house, try to get permission for the realtor in the group to give them a call or email to discuss the options using his/her services. I RARELY convert referrals where someone just gave somebody my name and number, they rarely call. Try to get the person providing the service or product to get in touch with the prospect if they'll take it. If you do this, you'll be far ahead of the rest of the group.

There are other events especially during the days in the form of luncheons, and expos, etc. It is vital that you make time to get out and continuously network so that you continue to drive new prospective clients into your marketing funnel.

Making the Most of Your One-on-One Networking Meetings with Other Professionals

When you're out networking you'll likely be in a group or attending an event with many people. It's possible to develop relationships and get more leads this way, but think of it as a process – especially if you are a member of a networking group.

You'll need to take it a step further to meet other members and professionals in the area in a one-on-one meeting. This allows you to get to know them and their business better, and vice versa. A lunch somewhere neutral but ideally at your facility, if you have one, is a start. You can offer to bring lunch for them so they can see your place and where you operate.

To maximize the potential value of such a meeting, which can easily deteriorate into shop talk, there are a few preliminary steps. Keeping on track is important, especially if you want to sound organized and professional.

A day or two before the meeting, send an email with a description of your target market and what kinds of leads you are seeking.
Keep it simple and clear. Be a giver! The more you give, the more you get.

Here's an example:

"Dear Mrs. Smith,
I will see you tomorrow at Panera Leesburg at 12 pm. If you have a few minutes when you get home, reply to this email with a description of who you are looking for as referral leads and I'll try to bring a couple of names to the meeting.

We are looking for more one-on-one clients or small groups of two or three people for reduced rate training. Our target market is a middle-aged person, most likely a women, married, with dual income who lives in or close to Ashburn. We also target business owners, busy professionals, and entrepreneurs as they are very busy and can benefit from our program. They would generally like a safe and time-efficient program (30 minutes).

If there's anything else I could help bring to the table please let me know.

Thank you."

At the meeting, stand and greet the person with a firm handshake. Review this simple outline to keep on track, maximize your time, and get the most out of your meeting.

1. Information about your businesses: Take turns offering some background and history about yourself and your business. Focus on current products or services. Keep it simple and offer your core service. Don't confuse them. You want them to remember you as the one who offers a particular service in your local area.

2. Target market: Let the other person know exactly what kind of lead or referral you are looking for and/or a description of your target market. The more descriptive the better for them. Also, let them know the best way for a lead or referral to contact you. Inform your colleague of your unique selling proposition. What makes you or your business better, cheaper, or different to that of your competitors?

3. Possible leads: Ideally, if you have a name or two with you, get the person you are meeting call the person who is the lead. You'll need to get their (the lead's) permission

to have your colleague give them a call or email. This is the best probability of turning it into a closed transaction. Try to have them do the same for you. We rarely convert leads when someone merely told them to call. Those people almost never call. You need to be proactive, get contact information for the lead you are given so that you can call yourself.

Follow up: If you can't bring leads to the meeting, don't stop there. Make a plan to reconnect with a phone call or email three to five days after you've had some time to digest your colleague's information and have looked through you contacts to see how you can find a match.

Follow this outline and you'll stay on track. It should only take an hour. You'll greatly increase both of your chances of obtaining more leads from your efforts. Hopefully, it will evolve into a long and lucrative relationship with fellow professionals in your area.

Develop Your Network and Prospects for New Business

Next to each job or industry listed below, write down the names and numbers or email of anyone you know, however remotely, in this industry. This is to establish your network and sphere of influence with people you currently know or with whom you have an association. Work backwards from an annual revenue goal with the prospecting goal setting worksheet.

Next, use the scripts below to call or email people (not cold calling, but business associates you already know) in your network who might know a good candidate for what you do. Follow-up scripts and lead qualification questions are also included.

Finally, use the daily call reporting worksheet below to keep track of your efforts.

We do this all the time, especially through email or other social media such as Facebook and LinkedIn with awesome results. Add this to your arsenal and teach it to your staff and they may have some good results over time.

A	J
Actor	Jeweler
Actuary	Jockey
Advertising	Joiner and Wood machinist
Advocate	Journalist
Aeronautical Engineer	
Aerospace Industry Trades	K
Agricultural Economist	Knitter
Agricultural Engineer	

Agricultural Extension Officer	L
Agricultural Inspector	Laborer
Agricultural Technician	Land Surveyor
Agriculture	Landscape Architect
Agriculturist	Law
Agronomist	Learner Official
Air Traffic Controller	Leather Chemist
Ambulance Emergency Care Worker	Leather Worker
Animal Scientist	Lecturer
Anthropologist	Librarian
Aquatic Scientist	Life-guard
Archaeologist	Lift Mechanic
Architect	Light Delivery Van Driver
Architectural Technologist	Linesman
Archivist	Locksmith
Area Manager	
	M
Armament Fitter	Machine Operator
Armature Winder	Machine Worker
Art Editor	Magistrate
Artist	Mail Handler
Assayer Sampler	Make-up Artist
Assembly Line Worker	Management Consultant
Assistant Draughtsman	Manager
Astronomer	Marine Biologist
Attorney	Marketing
Auctioneer	Marketing Manager
Auditor	Materials Engineer
Automotive Body Repairer	Mathematician
Automotive Electrician	Matron
Automotive Mechanic	Meat Cutting Technician
Automotive Trimmer	Mechanical Engineer
	Medical Doctor
B	Medical Orthotist Prosthetist
Babysitting Career	Medical Physicist
Banking Career	Merchandise Planner
Beer Brewing	Messenger
Biochemist	Meteorological Technician
Biokineticist	Meteorologist
Biologist	Meter-reader
Biomedical Engineer	Microbiologist
Biomedical Technologist	Miner
Blacksmith	Mine Surveyor
Boilermaker	Mining Engineer
Bookbinder	Model Builder
Bookkeeper	Model
Botanist	Motor Mechanic
Branch Manager	Musician
Bricklayer	
Bus Driver	N
Business Analyst	Nature Conservator
Business Economist	Navigating Officer
Butler	Navigator
	Nuclear Scientist
C	Nursing
Cabin Attendant	Nutritionist
Carpenter	
Cartographer	O
Cashier	Occupational Therapist
Ceramics Technologist	Oceanographer
Chartered Accountant	Operations Researcher
Chartered Management Accountant	Optical Dispenser
Chartered Secretary	Optical Technician

Chemical Engineer	Optometrist
Chemist	Ornithologist
Chiropractor	
City Treasurer	P
Civil Engineer	Painter and Decorator
Civil Investigator	Paint Technician
Cleaner	Paper Technologist
Clergyman	Patent Attorney
Clerk	Personal Trainer
Clinical Engineering	Personnel Consultant
Clinical Technologist	Petroleum Technologist
Clothing Designer	Pharmacist Assistant
Clothing Manager	Pharmacist
Coal Technologist	Photographer
Cobbler	Physicist
Committee Clerk	Physiologist
Computer Industry	Physiotherapist
Concrete Technician	Piano Tuner
Conservation and Wildlife	Pilot
Construction Manager	Plumber
Copy Writer	Podiatrist
Correctional Services	Police Officer
Costume Designer	Post Office Clerk
Crane Operator	Power Plant Operator
Credit Controller	Private Secretary
Crop Protection and Animal Health	Production Manager
Customer and Excise Officer	Projectionist
Customer Service Agent	Project Manager
	Psychologist
D	Psychometrist
Dancer	Public Relations Practitioner
Database Administrator	Purchasing Manager
Data Capturer	
Dealer in Oriental Carpets	Q
Decor Designer	Quality Control Inspector
Dental Assistant and Oral Hygienist	Quantity Surveyor
Dental Technician	
Dental Therapist	R
Dentist	Radiation Protectionist
Detective	Radio
Diamond Cutting	Radiographer
Diesel Fitter	Receptionist
Diesel loco Driver	Recreation Manager
Diesel Mechanic	Rigger
Die-sinker and Engraver	Road Construction Plant Operator
Dietician	Roofer
Diver	Rubber Technologist
DJ	
Domestic Appliance Mechanic	S
Domestic Personnel	Salesperson
Domestic radio and Television Mechanic	Sales Representative
Domestic Worker	Saw Operator
Draughtsman	Scale Fitter
Driver and Stacker	Sea Transport Worker
	Secretary
E	Security Officer
Earth Moving Equipment Mechanic	Sheetmetal Worker
Ecologist	Shop Assistant
Economist Technician	Shopfitter
Editor	Singer
Eeg Technician	Social Worker
Electrical and Electronic Engineer	Sociologist
Electrical Engineering Technician	Soil Scientist

The Entrepreneur Lifestyle

Electrician	Speech and Language Therapist
Electrician (Construction)	Sport Manager
Engineering	Spray Painter
Engineering Technician	Statistician
Entomologist	Swimming Pool Superintendent
Environmental Health Officer	Systems Analyst
Estate Agent	
Explosive Expert	T
Explosive Technologist	Tailor
Extractive Metallurgist	Taxidermist
	Teacher
F	Technical Illustrator
Farmer	Technical Writer
Farm Foreman	Teller
Farm Worker	Terminologist
Fashion Buyer	Textile Designer
Film and Production	Theatre Technology
Financial and Investment Manager	Tourism Manager
Fire-Fighter	Traffic Officer
Fireman at the Airport	Translator
Fitter and Turner	Travel Agent
Flight Engineer	Typist
Florist	
Food Scientist and Technologist	V
Footwear	Valuer and Appraiser
Forester Service	Vehicle Driver
Funeral Director	Veterinary Nurse
Furrier	Veterinary Surgeon
	Viticulturist
G	
Game Ranger	W
Gardener	Watchmaker
Geneticist	Weather Observer
Geographer	Weaver
Geologist	Welder
Geotechnologist	Wood Scientist
Goldsmith and Jeweler	Wood Technologist
Grain Grader	
Graphic Designer	Y
Gravure machine Minder	Yard Official
H	Z
Hairdresser	Zoologist
Herpetologist	
Home Economist	
Homoeopath	
Horticulturist	
Hospitality Industry	
Hospital Porter	
Human Resource Manager	
Hydrologist	
I	
Ichthyologist	
Industrial Designer	
Industrial Engineer	
Industrial Engineering Technologist	
Industrial Technician	
Inspector	
Instrument Maker	
Insurance	
Interior Designer	
Interpreter	

Inventory and Store Manager	

Prospecting Goal Setting

Work backwards from your annual income goal. Statistically, over a 12-month period, you should be on track to reach your goal.

Annual Income Goal: _____

Personal Income Per Deal: _____

Number of Deals Needed: _____

Monthly Deals Needed: _____

Consultations Needed/Deal: _____

Consultations Needed/Month: _____

Leads Needed/Consultation: _____

Leads Needed/Month: _____

Contacts Needed/Leads: _____

Contacts Needed/Month: _____

Days Worked/Month: _____

Contacts Needed/ Day: _____

Prospecting Script for Center of Influence

(Call people you know from your Market Development Inventory)

Hi, this is _____. This is a business call. Is this a good time to talk for a minute? Who do you know that could benefit from the type of training services we offer? Can you think of anyone in your (church group, family, neighborhood, or office) who may need my services at this time? Great! Would you mind if I gave them a call or email? By the way, do you currently work with a professional in this area? Terrific!

Client Just Signed Script (a day or two after sign-up)

Hi Mrs. Jones, this is_____ from (your company). Thank you again for coming in and signing up with us. I'm really excited about how you're going to do. While I'm thinking of it, most of the business we do is word of mouth. Do you know of anyone who would like to be part of or could benefit from our program as you're about to? Great! Would you mind if I gave them a call or email? Thank you very much!

Script for calling the prospect

Hi Mrs. Smith, my name is_____ from (your company). This is a sales call about our new program. Is this a good time? Your friend, Mrs. Jones, just signed up to join our program and mentioned your name as someone that might be interested in and could benefit from a program like this. Did you know we offer FREE consultations? Would you like to set one up? Which time is better for you, Monday at XXX pm or Tuesday at XXX pm? Great! Thanks for taking the time to speak with me. I'll see you Monday at XXX pm.

Pre-Qualify 100 per cent of prospects. You can mix these questions in smoothly upon the prospect's first call to you.

- How did you hear about me/us?
- What are you trying to achieve?
- Are you planning to interview more than one professional?
- Are you currently pursuing a solution on your own?
- Can you fit two or three meetings per week in your schedule?
- Is this 100 percent your decision or do you have to discuss this with somebody?
- If you feel this program is right for you, can you afford ($?$?$?) per session/month? Or ...
- My clients currently pay $60 per session. Does that work for you?
- If, after we meet you feel this is right for you, are you ready to start right away?

And, of course, keep track of your prospecting efforts to make sure you are staying on track for your annual goal.

Daily Call Reporting

Summary of Daily Total Numbers (from above):

Monday:
Contacts:_____
Consults:_____
Contracts:_____

Thursday:
Contacts:_____
Consults:_____
Contracts:_____

Tuesday:
Contacts: _____
Consults:_____
Contracts:_____

Friday:
Contacts:_____
Consults:_____
Contracts:_____

Wednesday:
Contacts:_____
Consults:_____
Contracts:_____

Weekly Totals:
Contacts:_____
Consults:_____
Contracts:_____

12 OPERATIONS

The key to operating efficiently is having documented and repeatable processes in your core service. Don't just fly by the seat of your pants every day. Some things will differ, but strive for organization and routine. If you were ever to hire someone else or sell your business, it should be easy for them to read your documentation and pick up your processes relatively easily in a day or two.

You should document all of your processes as you go. The idea is to come away with an operational manual that you could hand to someone else as if it's a cookbook of recipes for how your business runs. This will be helpful in the future if you have employees and managers or if you choose to sell your business down the road. Nobody wants to buy a discombobulated, unorganized business that they can't figure out how it runs. It will also serve to create more organization in your own day to day tasks.

We aren't talking about documenting all of the minutia of your busy day or any number of fires you have to put out that crop up at any given minute. What we do want to do is identify what your core processes are that you or staff perform on a consistent basis.

Create an outline of all of the ones you can list. Hopefully, there are not too many so your business is not too complex. It should be a relatively simple, repeatable process.

Once you have your outline of the major processes, add some finer detail bullet points underneath that describe the process. Expand on each bullet point with more thorough details to about a paragraph or two for each.

Put all of this together and in a binder and now you have an operational manual. It should be short and to the point that anyone can reference at any time. There is no secret information in here, nothing proprietary. Just your general, branded way of doing things daily. This is a manual you can keep behind the front desk for quick reference and staff training purposes.

Admin

Incorporation

Make sure to incorporate in your state by going to your state corporation commission or equivalent office. An LLC will most likely be the right choice for a single member company, but check with your attorney or accountant to be sure. Make sure to obtain a local county or town business license.

You'll need to call the IRS and obtain an EIN (employer identification number). This is like your business' social security number. You'll need it to open your business bank account later. Be sure to obtain any trademarks either state or national that might be pertinent to your business logo, slogan, etc. Be certain that you determine if you will have employees or contractors. Don't make the mistake of hiring people as contractors when they are really employees. You could end up owing back taxes. You can view the IRS' page on how to determine who is an employee and who is a contractor.
http://www.irs.gov/Businesses/Small-Businesses-&-Self-Employed/Independent-Contractor-Self-Employed-or-Employee

Naming your business. You'll want to name your business something that is descriptive of what you do or offer and reflects your personal brand. The same is true for your logo design. To operate under a different business name or a shortened one (like S.P.A.R.T.A.) you can file a simple DBA, Doing Business As, form with your state corporation commission. You may need to do this so that you do not have to use the

LLC at the end of your name if you chose to incorporate as a limited liability company. More on this shortly.

Legal

If you can afford it, find an attorney and pay him a retainer to become a client when legal issues arise. Or at the very least, create a list of people you could call when legal issues come up. Additionally, some services like Pre-paid Legal or maybe even Legal Zoom can offer some peace of mind and help solve smaller more routine legal issues should they arise. Your local small business attorneys may offer similar services. Contact them through your local organizations.

To get you started, download this list of over
600 commonly used business and personal legal forms.
http://goo.gl/5M1Oyc

Leasing/Buying Commercial Space

If you'll be working in your own studio or health club, you'll need to lease or buy space. There are a lot of mistakes that can be made in this process. What if it is on the second floor? Can you even get your heavy equipment up there? Those kinds of things will have to be taken into consideration as well as more legal and political considerations having to do with operating a business in your local area. Use the worksheet below to properly identify all the factors that will be relevant to your business operating in your area.

Office Lease Check list

Property:_____ Date Viewed:_____
Rent:_____ Sq. Ft:_____
Lease Term:_____ When Available:_____
Payment Due Date:_____ Contract Available:_____
Deposit:_____ Parking Availability:____
Security in Place:_____ Structural Insurance:____

Utilities: Use of:
  - Water/Power/AC: - Conference Room:

- Phone: - Bathroom/change:
- Internet: - Kitchen:

Access by Employees after hours/weekends:

Lease Restrictions/Zoning:

Floor wt. restrictions:

Early Termination of Lease by Tenant:

Early Termination of Lease by Landlord:

Option to Renew:

Modifications to Office:

Remedy for Service Interruption:

Responsibility for Repairs:

Conditions for Return of Property:

Specifications for Signs:

Client Database Templates

To keep track of your client's information, you'll need to include them in a database and manage it going forward. This is useful if you don't use a system like <u>our all in one business software http://bit.ly/1XajCj4</u> which includes a customer relationship manager (CRM).

These two excel spreadsheets can help you manage this information. One is simpler with minimal client information and the other is much more detailed.

<u>Client database contact list http://goo.gl/C4nXeR</u>
<u>Client database template http://goo.gl/4Kkx0o</u>

Staff Meetings

If you have staff, you will most certainly have the need for meetings. In the corporate world, meetings, in many cases, are massive wastes of time that are inefficient and don't accomplish much. We're not going to do that. If you're not meeting, your staff is probably not all on the same page. Things change and you all need to stay together. Your staff may not see the need or value in weekly meetings, but it is absolutely critical that they stay up to date on important things like your pricing, what promotions you have going on, and any ongoing educational information you provide. If they don't take it seriously and don't show up on time, if at all, they are not right for your company. Be certain to convey the importance of showing up to and participating in meetings.

You will have three types of meetings. Possibly four. Weekly staff meetings. Quarterly staff/leadership/management meetings. Annual meetings that include everyone. The fourth option is an emergency mandatory meeting you can call at any time. But, we won't focus on that right now.

Let's work backwards and start with your annual meeting. January may not make sense to have it at the start of the calendar year. You will want to have a plan and promotions in place well before the new year gets there. It may make more sense to have your annual meeting in the middle of Summer when things may be slower. Alternatively, you could have it closer to the holidays so your most important promotions for the holidays and new year are more fresh in everyone's mind. The choice is your's.

Your annual meeting should last all day. You will have a lot to cover for your strategy and plan for the entire year. This is when you'll reconfirm or reestablish your company vision and mission. What is decided here may change the business plan.
You may want to have part of the day for everyone and part of the day just for leadership and management after employees have left.

Quarterly, or every 90 days, you will want to have a slightly different meeting. Large businesses run on 90 time tables and that is how their numbers are measured and reported. You should do the same. Begin by reviewing the previous quarter's goals and results. Establish the upcoming quarter's goals. And solve any ongoing problems. This meeting might also last all day. It will last all day for leadership and maybe half the day for employees.

Weekly meetings are really about the staff. These meetings can last anywhere from 60-90 minutes. Begin with a review of anything relevant that happened over the last week. Everyone is free to contribute. Review your numbers, particularly your marketing numbers, but especially your sales numbers. Make sure everyone is on track with their individual numbers and goals. Solve any problems that have arisen in the last week. Use this time to review and check on customer attitude and satisfaction as well as employees. Write down a handful of action items for each person to accomplish by the following week. Use the remainder of the time to address any weekly staff training or educational materials like business books read together or more technical training information being consumed as a team.

Be sure to start this meeting on time and don't let it run over. Getting out of this habit can eat up valuable weekly time. If someone is late, start without them, but document it as one strike against them. They will have to catch up later at their own expense. Review the action items for each person and conclude the meeting. Wednesdays or Thursdays around mid-morning or lunch time seem to be good days for businesses to have these types of meetings.

Problem Solving

Without question problems are going to come up weekly if not daily. It's important that staff members bring these to the weekly meeting. Identify the real source of the problem, get multiple perspectives on the same problem and discuss all the possible solutions. Get input from everyone if necessary. If everyone agrees, go with that solution. If there is disagreement, leadership will determine the best course of action to take. Don't leave a weekly meeting without solving or knowing what to do to solve any issues. Decisiveness is good in business. Any decision is better than no decision at all. Even if it is a total failure, you will know sooner than had you waited and done nothing. It will still give you more time to correct it once you know it was the wrong course of action.

Developing Systematized Training Manuals

One of the easiest systems for any business to put in place is by creating training manuals. These don't have to be huge at all, but they do need to be well written and easy to understand. Plus they must be kept up to date, if not they are useless.

A good training manual is one that teaches the reader how to follow a process from the beginning to the end. No step should be left out, and it should include tips on rectifying issues should they occur. Think of a cookbook. It's essentially a recipe for some specific process in your business you're creating that anyone should be able to pick up, read, and replicate without trouble.

The best way to write or develop your training manual is to document each step. This will take time and effort, and no doubt, small steps will be left out. This will be because the person doing the task is so familiar with it, they will leave out obvious things.

The whole trick to a good training manual is to not leave out those small items. Once the first draft of the manual has been prepared hand it over to someone who is unfamiliar with the process. Then see if they can complete the task without any help. If they can your manual is finished, if not go back in and make revisions until anyone can do the process.

Templates are another easy way to systemize your business. You can use templates for all kinds of tasks including emails, newsletters, business letters, sales letters, short processes and more.

A template is a fill in the blanks type of document that just needs updating. It is a great tool to use for writing sales messages or product releases. Plus they can be handed to anyone with simple instructions on how to complete them.

A customer service training manual is an excellent business tool to have. This way you can ensure that all of your customer service representatives are following the same procedures. All support tickets or customer calls will be handled professionally and have that company stamp to them.

The biggest issue with training manuals is keeping them up to date. If your company is large then you can easily assign one person this responsibility. On average each training manual should be reviewed about every six months. If new tools or software are used, then add updating manuals to one of your templates.

Creating and developing new training manuals can be time consuming. Try to keep it simple. Follow an outline. Once they are in place, however, you will appreciate their full benefit. Your company will be more streamlined than ever before.

IT

Website-Wordpress

If you can afford to work with a reputable and reliable web developer, go ahead and do it. Probably your best bet for being visible on the web is setting yourself up a Wordpress blog. www.wordpress.org. It serves as your website and a content management system that you can easily update and manage yourself on a regular basis.

Regular posts on your blog will help the search engines bring your site up higher in results with the more recent and relevant content that you add. Additionally, there are many plug-ins and different themes to use to customize it. More than one income stream can be created by creating membership areas or selling other products through your site. You can even hide things behind a password protected page or post on your site. If you use some of the resources listed earlier like Paypal and Google Checkout, you can easily place the code for payment buttons on your site to take payments not only from your local customers, but from potential customers all over the world. We'll go more into other income streams later.

But, understand this. Starting a business is, most of the time, focusing on the local market. With tools like the internet, now you have the opportunity to scale up your business in numerous other ways, to disseminate your knowledge beyond your local community, and potentially become an international presence.

It's best to be simple at first and expand from there. A $10,000 website won't do you any good if you don't have any clients or it's not getting you any clients. There is absolutely nothing wrong with investing in professional looking graphics and a website. But, be careful and tread lightly here. Many people I know have been burned by the unprofessional in the web development/design arena. The good thing about a Wordpress site is it can be very basic and you can ramp it up to infinite complexity from there without the need to change much or redo an entire site. You can manage content yourself easily.

At the very least, you'll want your site to market you or your business with who you are, what you do, where you're located, and why potential clients should choose you. Make sure you include a call to action for them to DO something before they leave your page. Either opt-in to your email list through your web form (that you get through Aweber or **our all in one business software** http://bit.ly/1XajCj4 which sits on your home page. Or that they should call you to set up a free consultation. Attach some kind of time sensitive promotion to initiate action from them.

When you do post, some things work better than others. Most people don't sit down to read a long blog post anymore. It's more of a skimming activity. You want several things that will increase the likelihood a reader will consume your information. You'll want an attention grabbing headline. Something that is interesting or invokes an emotional response in the potential reader. Within the first and last line of the post, you will probably want to include your keywords and phrases you target. Be sure to create an in text link back to your home page or to some other post on your site on the topic. Use multiple sub headlines, bullets, or numbers to highlight the major points of the post and to catch a skimming eye. Pictures with captions can also catch a skimming eye and drive the point home better. Better still, is a short video you can create to be embedded directly in the post. It is potentially a better way for the person to get the information rather than reading it, but you'll also pull traffic in from a different source like YouTube if that's where you uploaded it. All of those things contribute to better search results and the chance the reader will actually read or watch your information provided.

To accompany this chapter, check out this **10-part video training series on how to build a better business blog.**

[Click here to download How to Build a Better Business Blog](http://goo.gl/WbZRqj).
http://goo.gl/WbZRqj

Customer Service

The Customer Always Comes First

Let's talk a little about some simple yet effective strategies that will help you provide excellent customer service for your business.

Did you know that customer service is often an under-valued aspect of doing business? When in fact, if you want your business to be successful, you need to train yourself and your employees to understand that the customer must always come first.

When it comes to providing good customer service it is important to personalize your approach as much as possible. One thing all customers have in common is the pleasure they receive when establishments they patronize make it clear to them that they know who they all are.

You have to prove to your customers that you appreciate them. You can do this by addressing them by name during all of your communications with them. The golden rule is; make them feel important and they'll prove that you're important to them, too!

Always give your best plus more

You should train your employees to go the extra mile for the customers as well. Being respectful and smiling at all times may seem like a little thing but it can go a long way towards improving your business's customer service record. Remember, it's often these little things that make a big difference to your customers.

Always be fair

No request should be too small to be considered, and no customer should be too insignificant to take care of. Sure, there are certain privileges that VIP customers are entitled to and other customers are quick to understand, but there are also certain privileges that everyone has the right to enjoy like common courtesy and dedication. Never let your customers think that you're guilty of favoritism!

Make sure you listen

It is extremely important that you listen to what your customers have to say. This may be hard when the customer is stubborn and unreasonable. Even if you end up unable to resolve the issue, your customers should still put the phone down in a good mood because they knew you cared enough to listen to them without confrontation.

Make good use of FAQ's

If you don't have a frequently asked questions file or webpage for your business, create one immediately. Having a FAQ page is an effective way of offering good customer service on the fly. Keep a record of common questions and problems that have been discussed for quick reference. This will help to negate the need for repeat calls regarding the same issues. FAQ sections can help prevent your customers and employees from wasting their time.

Never leave issues unresolved

Every complaint must be successfully addressed. Train your employees to perform follow-up calls to ensure that all complaints had been resolved. For complicated issues, make sure that you give customers progress reports to let them know that you're still working on their case. Do your best to give them a specific time period for which they can expect the issue to be fully resolved.
These are just a few basic strategies that you can use to beef up customer service for your own business. Follow them and you will be well on your way to providing excellent service to all of your customers.

We have a lot to go over in the next few chapters. If you want to learn how to provide the best customer service for your business, make sure you keep reading and take in everything in the rest of this book. We will be talking about some simple secrets to providing great customer service all of the time!

Your Bread and Butter

In this chapter we are going to go over some simple secrets to providing great customer service all of the time.

It is no secret that if you are in the service industry, good customer service can be your bread and butter. By providing good customer service, you can generate more profit and promote business loyalty at the same time.

In fact, it can create a win-win scenario for both the business and the customer. The customers have a good experience and get their money's worth while the business gets to enjoy increased profits!

Let's go over a few simple secrets that you can use for your own business.

Strive to build customer loyalty

Customer loyalty is the most important secret to achieve good customer service. Do your best to collect your customer's full name, contact numbers and other information, such as address, birth date etc.

Remember if you show concern for what matters to your customers, you will build their loyalty and acquiring customers for life.

Provide authentic customer service

Nowadays, service has been a cliche and just a traditional way of dealing with customers. If everyone's doing it, it's a high time that you personalize your service. Be creative; personally know your customers and identify their individual needs. Make certain that your offer extreme value to your customers.

The customer is always right

The old adage "customer is always right" is still applicable. If a customer approaches you and complains, be serious when handling their concern. It can take a lot of guts to come to you and express concern. Most people will just not say anything. If you're getting feedback at all, you're one step ahead in solving a potential issue. If the customer is angry and upset, do your best to defuse the situation and show them how serious you are when it comes correcting any problems.

Once the customer is satisfied by how you addressed their complaint, thank them for conveying the problem to you. Keep in mind that advertising will not be enough to repair a damage done by failing to address customer complaints. Silent complainers can do a great deal of damage to your business. Beware of people who walk away without having their issue resolved. You may never see them again, if they are unhappy you can bet that they are openly criticizing your services to other people and establishing a bad reputation for your business.

Be honest with the customers

Once your customer suspects that you are lying to them, they are a lost buyer. If a customer seeks your advice about your service, openly tell them what they need to know. In the end, they will thank you for being so genuine with what you offer.

Go the extra mile

If you want superb customer service, you should always go the extra mile. For instance you can send a birthday card or a thank you note. You can send a congratulatory note when a customer gets promoted or you can clip the article if you see their photo or names in print. There are many ways to encourage your customers lifetime loyalty. You just have to be willing to make the effort.

Train your staff well

Educate and train them about good customer service and your way of doing things. There will be times when you can't directly deal with your customers and your staff must be able to show them the excellent customer service that they want.

Always keep in mind that your competitors are just waiting to cater unsatisfied customers of yours so you should always be sure to take care of your customer by providing good customer service.
That's it for today's lesson. Look for another lesson soon! We will be talking about customer service training with three quick steps.

Training for Customer Service

In this chapter we are going to talk about three quick steps to effective customer service training.

Did you know that effective customer service training can be done in three quick steps? Once your employees have completed the training course you can rest assured that your business will benefit and enjoy increased revenues as well a bigger and more loyal customer base.

Let's jump right in to the steps you should take when training your employees to provide top notch customer service.

Step 1 - Prepare materials and tools for customer service training.

Be as detailed and specific as you can when composing materials for customer service training. It is imperative that your employees understand what you think good customer service should be. Give them concrete examples of acceptable and unacceptable behavior and steps to take in given situations. Provide them with a list of do's and don'ts to remember.

Secondly, help them understand why offering good customer service is important to the business and how it will ultimately affect them as well. Employees will be more motivated to improve their customer service skills if they believe that doing so is beneficial to them as well.

Prepare scripts for common customer service issues. This will ensure that your customer service team will be able to deliver a speedy and uniform response to your customers. Determine your desired response schedule and make sure that the training materials are designed to help them comply with the desired response time.

Step 2 - Take all the time you need to train your staff.

Focus on one lesson at a time and don't progress to another level until you're sure that they've mastered their lessons. It is a good idea to hold periodical tests to ensure that they continue to retain knowledge from your previous lessons.
Let them take a gradual approach to their new set of responsibilities. Have them start with something small and relatively easy like handling routine customer service calls. Always clarify their job duties and the level of authority they're working with before allowing them to interact with the customers.

Last but not the least, remind them to consult your FAQ section (and to help the clients find it) before delving in to more complicated processes of resolution.

Step 3 - Monitor the performance of your customer service team.

Subject your employees to scheduled and spontaneous simulations to give you a chance to evaluate their response in critical situations.

Make sure that you provide them feedback afterwards, identifying their strengths, weaknesses and offering suggestions for improvements.

You may even consider developing an incentive program to further motivate your employees and encourage them to always be on their best behavior when interacting with customers. It is also important to evaluate your employee's customer service abilities on a regular basis.

Always be prepared to make changes with how you run your customer service team. Remember they're the ones that are directly interacting with your customers, so your team and its policies must be flexible in order to respond quickly to a customer's needs.

Customer Service Surveys

We still need to go over a few things about how to provide good customer service for your business. We are going to jump right into how to make a good customer service survey. As we have been discussing throughout this series, customer service is a way to communicate with the customers by providing assistance about the service and the most vital aspect in evaluating the customer's satisfaction is through customer service.

Many business owners don't realize that good customer service creates happy, satisfied, repeat customers. One way to measure the customer service standards for any business is through customer surveys. This is a vital tool that is often overlooked.

A customer service survey shows the solid reputation of the business you have established. Customers have the chance to evaluate whether their expectations are met and if they have been treated well by the business.

Through customer service surveys, positive and negative remarks are clearly shown. Basically this is just a simple way of getting feedback from your valued customers.

This information allows the business to evaluate their standards and develop better customer service policies. Customer service surveys can also help when it comes to making good business decisions.

A well written customer survey can give you all of the information that you need to make positive changes in your business. On the other hand surveys that aren't well written will not help you achieve the results that you want. To avoid this it is important that you follow a few simple guidelines to craft an effective survey questionnaire.

Identify your objectives

The survey objectives are very important; carefully identify your specific objectives. When goals are not clear you will end up with a questionnaire that is unfocused and ineffective. Always be direct about the information you want to acquire. Successful surveys act as tools in denying and confirming the customer's expectation's from your business.

Questions in the survey must be easily answered. Customers don't want to have a hard time answering your questions. Never use abbreviations, slang or any technical jargon in your questionnaire. You will obtain more helpful answers if you make the questions easy.

When it comes to crafting a good survey you can use a few different types of questions, such as:

- Questions answered with a simple yes or no.

(For example: Will you purchase this service again?)
- Questions answered by multiple choices.

(For example: Which products do you like most? Product A, B. or C?)
- You can also use scale or rankings and ask the customer to rate their experience.

(For example: Please rate our service from 1 to 5). Be sure to identify which end of the scale is low or high with regard to satisfaction.
- Use open ended questions.(For example: What are your suggestions to better improve our services?
- Alternate your questions.

Try mixing easy and difficult questions throughout your survey. This will help keep the customers interested and encourage them to answer more questions. A good rule of thumb is to set two easy questions first, like the yes or no and the multiple choice questions. Then start to include your open ended questions. This process will keep your customers from feeling like you are requesting too much from them. You can also use this little trick to make sure you are getting truthful answers. You can ask the same question in different ways a few questions apart. It will seem like a different question, to the survey taker, but will give you the information you are looking for. If the survey taker is being truthful, you should get the same answer in different forms for both questions. If they conflict, you'll be forced to think something isn't right with their feedback and start to look at the other information they provided.

Don't be biased

Lastly don't make the questions biased. Successful surveys should get the true opinion of the customer and not just the answers that you want to hear. This is the best way to measure customer satisfaction. Encourage the responders to be honest. Sometimes negative criticism is your best friend.

Along with not being biased, you want to use the preceding strategies and more to make sure that what you are trying to measure or receive as feedback is what you are actually measuring. You can just simply ask what clients want. You also have to observe what is implicit in their actions and recognize that it might be different from what they say.

Customer service surveys are a very important tool that can help you make informed decisions for the betterment your business, products and services. If your goal is to achieve a 100% satisfaction rating from your customers, using surveys will definitely help you to achieve that goal. You can also let them know that you will be keeping answers anonymous so there will be less inhibition on their part in filling out the survey. Of course, if you need to know who answers what questions, this strategy won't work.
One last point. The total effort clients should put into a survey should be very short. No more than 5 or 10 minutes max. If it's too complicated or too long, they'll be less likely to do it again in the future. Compensating them for their time in some way will help slightly. It doesn't have to be anything expensive, just something recognizing their effort. It could be a free session, a discount on another service you offer, a discounted renewal rate, a gift card to another service or business they like. Your options are endless here. Use your imagination, but thank your clients for their effort and feedback.

Tips for Achieving Superb Customer Service

In this chapter we are going to go over some great tips for achieving superb customer service ratings.

Over the last few lessons we have talked a lot about customer loyalty. One of the most important factors in attaining and keeping customer loyalty is to respect the people aspect of your business. Treating customers as individuals and not just as a representation of financial profits can give you a big competitive edge. This becomes harder to do the larger your company gets.

I remember one of my former bosses decided to come to a networking lunch that I attended regularly. He sat down next to a long time member of the group who had also become one of my clients recently. My boss introduced himself to the gentleman and the man replied "I know, I'm one of your customers." That's not a good feeling for a client.

As we have learned during this book, good customer service is a vital part of any business. When it comes to achieving great customer service ratings it is important to keep these simple tips in mind:

Happy employee's make for happy customers

Keep in mind that there is no way to provide quality customer service without the qualified people providing it. Having excited and engaged employees is a great way to ensure good customer service. Choose them wisely to begin with, pay your employees fair wages; give them good benefits and train them well. This will allow them to exude confidence when dealing with customers and will naturally lead to better customer service.

Be a good role model

Always remember that the way you treat your employees will be reflective of how they treat your customers. You are their role model so always be the epitome of a good service provider.

Greet your employees enthusiastically every day and listen when they speak. Rude customer service is not always a reflection of the employees' attitudes but also of their employer. Foster a positive culture.

Know your customers

And let them get to know you. Recognizing your customers and calling them by their names are indications that you really know them. They will feel important by this simple gesture. Additionally, by letting them know who you are, they can also feel comfortable that they can reach you easily when problems arise.

Be pleasant

Give pleasant greetings when your customers walk in the door or contact you. Greetings are important part of customer service and will let the customers know that they are respected, valued, and appreciated. Call them by name and always try to go a little above and beyond the call of your obligated duties for them.

Provide proper training

As we discussed before, give your employees proper training on how to handle customer complaints. Guidelines must be set on what to do and say in each conceivable case. Front liners play the most important role in the customer's experience. Be sure that your staff knows what to say and do to create a more positive and pleasant customer experience.

Don't forget to survey

Devise a "What do you think of our business" survey. Create a short and simple questionnaire with questions like we discussed in your last lesson. For example; find out what your customers don't like, what should be changed and what should be done to provide better service. The answers to these questions will be very useful in creating your customer service plan, since your customers will be the ones making the suggestions. Make sure you take note of all of the important points and act on them.
The questionnaire can help you anticipate and identify customer needs. This may sound odd, but customers don't usually buy products and services. They buy good feelings and solutions to their problems. Most customers are emotional rather than logical. It is important to anticipate their needs by talking to them regularly. This way, you can be aware of their problems and you can take care of their upcoming needs.

Customer service is an important part of any business and it should be viewed as a natural extension of the business. Always remember that the customer is the most essential asset of your business and without them, your business will not exist. Keep them happy and satisfied by providing superb customer service and you will reap the rewards.

Retention

Everyone is always interested in more clients and making more money. However, many people fail to realize that the real money is going to come from the current clientele that you already have. It will come in the form of referrals from those happy people, but specifically, the repeat business of those happy clients. Hopefully, if you've done everything right, they will be more than happy. They won' t be able to shut up about you. Above, we talked about some general customer service concepts. Let's get into some retention specifics.

To start off with, you'll want to be certain you have the basics down.

- Always showing up on time or a few minutes early to properly prepare for any appointment. Never make people wait on you.
- Return all phone calls and messages (including text and email) in a timely manner.
- Follow up if you say you will in a timely manner.
- Don't cancel.

That alone can set you apart from many of the people using bad business practices out there. Let's take it a step further.

- Greet clients appropriately every time they come in.
- Give firm handshakes with eye contact. Both for men and women. Don't get caught up in treating people differently based on who they are.
- Engage in some small talk. Ask about family, recent or upcoming vacations, career developments for them.
- Offer a simple, small, healthful breakfast or snack for early morning clients.
- Be empathetic and supportive if they are under stress.
- Angle your appointments toward feeling positive, but accomplishing a goal too.
- Let your sense of humor be seen.
- Don't dump your personal problems on them. You can relay that you understand and have experienced the same as them, but attempt to support and do something to improve rather than spreading misery around.
- Be confident, but humble, not cocky.
- Be on your game energy wise all the time. You are human too, but nobody wants to work with someone who is half asleep because they are tired.
- Be sure to recognize good efforts as they occur. Praise.
- Talk with your client in the last few minutes of an appointment. Keep it light. Keep it positive or focused on something to do for next time. May include small talk or personal things again.
- Have free refreshments available.
- Personal discussions are fine, just know your boundaries.

You should stay in contact with your clients outside of a few minutes a week with you, in person.

- If you have a break after a client, offer to buy them a coffee.
- Recognition is very important. A simple text recognizing a good effort or some other small accomplishment can go a long way.
- Regularly send educational information in email. Preferably once weekly. It helps if relevant to your clients' perceived issues.
- Offer to take clients out to lunch. You have to eat and it's a business expense. It allows you to get to know them better and connect on a deeper level.
- If your clients depend on referrals, always try to make connections for them that could result in more business.
- Reward your clients for referrals to you.
  - Remembering birthdays and other important dates can go a long way. Bonus if you send a card. You can use a management system like **our all in one business software** http://bit.ly/1XajCj4 for this.
- Know your client's family member names.
- Know how old they are.
- Know where they work.
- If you get invited to parties, go.
- Invite clients to social outings.
- Organize social gatherings for your clients at your facility or another location. Instills more of a community attitude. And can be a great networking opportunity. Bonus if you encourage them to bring a friend who may be a good lead for you.
- People do business with their friends and who they know, like, and trust. Be that person.
- Make them smile, surprise them.
- Hold yourself accountable for delivering what you say you will.
- Preserve your word and integrity.
- If conflicts arise, keep your emotions out of it.
- Do what you need to do to diffuse and make it right as quickly as possible.

If you're priced right and have a high margin, none of these things should have a burdensome feeling for you. In fact, you may not be able to afford NOT doing them. They should help repay you in dividends in the form of repeat business.

I sincerely hope that you have learned a lot about how to provide good customer service in your personal training business!

13 FINANCE

Now to what can be argued as the heart of every business. Unless you have a traditional finance education, this is one area that is often most confusing for many entrepreneurs if not being an area they don't want to deal with at all. Fear not, we will go over an in depth financial education you can understand to help your business run in a healthy manner.

What Is Accounting Anyway?

Anyone who's worked in an office at some point or another has had to go to accounting. They're the people who pay and send out the bills that keep the business running. They do a lot more than that, though. Sometimes referred to as "bean counters" they also keep their eye on profits, costs and losses. Unless you're running your own business and acting as your own accountant, you'd have no way of knowing just how profitable - or not - your business is without some form of accounting.

No matter what business you're in, even if all you do is balance a checkbook, that's still accounting. It's part of even a kid's life. Saving an allowance, spending it all at once - these are accounting principles.

What are some other businesses where accounting is critical? Well, farmers need to follow careful accounting procedures. Many of them run their farms year to year by taking loans to plant the crops. If it's a good year, a profitable one, then they can pay off their loan; if not, they might have to carry the loan over, and accrue more interest charges.

Every business and every individual needs to have some kind of accounting system in their lives. Otherwise, the finances can get away from them, they don't know what they've spent, or whether they can expect a profit or a loss from their business. Staying on top of accounting, whether it's for a multi-billion dollar business or for a personal checking account is a necessary activity on a daily basis if you're smart. Not doing so can mean anything from a bounced check or posting a loss to a company's shareholders. Both scenarios can be equally devastating.

Accounting is basically information, and this information is published periodically in business as a profit and loss statement, or an income statement.

Basic Accounting Principles

Accounting has been defined as, by Professor of Accounting at the University of Michigan William A Paton as having one basic function: "facilitating the administration of economic activity. This function has two closely related phases: 1) measuring and arraying economic data; and 2) communicating the results of this process to interested parties."

As an example, a company's accountants periodically measure the profit and loss for a month, a quarter or a fiscal year and publish these results in a statement of profit and loss that's called an income statement. These statements include elements such as accounts receivable (what's owed to the company) and accounts payable (what the company owes). It can also get pretty complicated with subjects like retained earnings and accelerated depreciation. This at the higher levels of accounting and in the organization.

Much of accounting though, is also concerned with basic bookkeeping. This is the process that records every transaction; every bill paid, every dime owed, every dollar and cent spent and accumulated.

But the owners of the company, which can be individual owners or millions of shareholders are most concerned with the summaries of these transactions, contained in the financial statement. The financial statement summarizes a company's assets. A value of an asset is what it cost when it was first acquired. The financial statement also records what the sources of the assets were. Some assets are in the form of loans that have to be paid back. Profits are also an asset of the business.

In what's called double-entry bookkeeping, the liabilities are also summarized. Obviously, a company wants to show a higher amount of assets to offset the liabilities and show a profit. The management of these two elements is the essence of accounting.

There is a system for doing this; not every company or individual can devise their own systems for accounting; the result would be chaos!

Accounting Principles

If everyone involved in the process of accounting followed their own system, or no system at all, there's be no way to truly tell whether a company was profitable or not. Most companies follow what are called generally accepted accounting principles, or GAAP, and there are huge tomes in libraries and bookstores devoted to just this one topic. Unless a company states otherwise, anyone reading a financial statement can make the assumption that company has used GAAP.

If GAAP are not the principles used for preparing financial statements, then a business needs to make clear which other form of accounting they're used and are bound to avoid using titles in its financial statements that could mislead the person examining it. GAAP are the gold standard for preparing financial statement. Not disclosing that it has used principles other than GAAP makes a company legally liable for any misleading or misunderstood data. These principles have been fine-tuned over decades and have effectively governed accounting methods and the financial reporting systems of businesses. Different principles have been established for different types of business entities, such for-profit and not-for-profit companies, governments and other enterprises.

GAAP are not cut and dried, however. They're guidelines and as such are often open to interpretation. Estimates have to be made at times, and they require good faith efforts towards accuracy. You've surely heard the phrase "creative accounting" and this is when a company pushes the envelope a little (or a lot) to make their business look more profitable than it might actually be. This is also called massaging the numbers. This can get out of control and quickly turn into accounting fraud, which is also called cooking the books. The results of these practices can be devastating and ruin hundreds and thousands of lives, as in the cases of Enron, Rite Aid and others.

Bookkeeping

So what goes on the accounting and bookkeeping departments? What do these people do on a daily basis?

Well, one thing they do that's terribly important to everyone working there is Payroll. All the salaries and taxes earned and paid by every employee every pay period have to be recorded. The payroll department has to ensure that the appropriate federal, state and local taxes are being deducted. The pay stub attached to your paycheck records these taxes. They usually include income tax, social security taxes pous employment taxes that have to be paid to federal and state government. Other deductions include personal ones, such as for retirement, vacation, sick pay or medical benefits. It's a critical function. Some companies have their own payroll departments; others outsource it to specialists.

The accounting department receives and records any payments or cash received from customers or clients of the business or service. The accounting department has to make sure that the money is sourced accurately and deposited in the appropriate accounts. They also manage where the money goes; how much of it is kept on-hand for areas such as payroll, or how much of it goes out to pay what the company owes its banks, vendors and other obligations. Some should also be invested.

The other side of the receivables business is the payables area, or cash disbursements. A company writes a lot of checks during the course of year to pay for purchases, supplies, salaries, taxes, loans and services. The accounting department prepares all these checks and records to whom they were disbursed, how much and for what. Accounting departments also keep track of purchase orders placed for inventory, such as products that will be sold to customers or clients. They also keep track of assets such as a business's property and equipment. This can include the office building, furniture, computers, even the smallest items such as pencils and pens.

Profit and Loss

It might seem like a no-brainer to define just exactly what profit and loss are. But of course these have definitions like everything else. Profit can be called different things, for a start. It's sometimes called net income or net earnings. Businesses that sell products and services generate profit from the sales of those products or services and from controlling the attendant costs of running the business. Profit can also be referred to as Return on Investment, or ROI. While some definitions limit ROI to profit on investments in such securities as stocks or bonds, many companies use this term to refer to short-term and long-term business results. Profit is also sometimes called taxable income.

It's the job of the accounting and finance professionals to assess the profits and losses of a company. They have to know what created both and what the results of both sides of the business equation are. They determine what the net worth of a company is. Net worth is the resulting dollar amount from deducting a company's liabilities from its assets. In a privately held company, this is also called owner's equity, since anything that's left over after all the bills are paid, to put it simply, belongs to the owners. In a publicly held company, this profit is returned to the shareholders in the form of dividends. In other words, all liabilities have the first claim on any money the company makes. Anything that's left over is profit. It's not derived from one element or another. Net worth is determined after all the liabilities are deducted from all the assets, including cash and property.

Showing a profit, or a positive figure on the balance sheet, is of course the aim of every business. It's what our economy and society are built on. It doesn't always work out that way. Economic trends and consumer behaviors change and it's not always possible to predict these and what income they'll have on a company's performance.

Bookkeeping Basics

Most people probably think of bookkeeping and accounting as the same thing, but bookkeeping is really one function of accounting, while accounting encompasses many functions involved in managing the financial affairs of a business. Accountants prepare reports based, in part, on the work of bookkeepers.

Bookkeepers perform all manner of record-keeping tasks. Some of them include the following:

-They prepare what are referred to as source documents for all the operations of a business - the buying, selling, transferring, paying and collecting. The documents include papers such as purchase orders, invoices, credit card slips, time cards, time sheets and expense reports. Bookkeepers also determine and enter in the source documents what are called the financial effects of the transactions and other business events. Those include paying the employees, making sales, borrowing money or buying products or raw materials for production.

-Bookkeepers also make entries of the financial effects into journals and accounts. These are two different things. A journal is the record of transactions in chronological order. An accounts is a separate record, or page for each asset and each liability. One transaction can affect several accounts.

-Bookkeepers prepare reports at the end of specific period of time, such as daily, weekly, monthly, quarterly or annually. To do this, all the accounts need to be up to date. Inventory records must be updated and the reports checked and double-checked to ensure that they're as error-free as possible.
-The bookkeepers also compile complete listings of all accounts. This is called the adjusted trial balance. While a small business may have a hundred or so accounts, very large businesses can have more than 10,000 accounts.

-The final step is for the bookkeeper to close the books, which means bringing all the bookkeeping for a fiscal year to a close and summarized.

Personal Accounting

If you have a checking account, of course you balance it periodically to account for any differences between what's in your statement and what you wrote down for checks and deposits. Many people do it once a month when their statement is mailed to them, but with the advent of online banking, you can do it daily if you're the sort whose banking tends to get away from them.

You balance your checkbook to note any charges in your checking account that you haven't recorded in your checkbook. Some of these can include ATM fees, overdraft fees, special transaction fees or low balance fees, if you're required to keep a minimum balance in your account. You also balance your checkbook to record any credits that you haven't noted previously. They might include automatic deposits, or refunds or other electronic deposits. Your checking account might be an interest-bearing account and you want to record any interest that it's earned.

You also need to discover if you've made any errors in your recordkeeping or if the bank has made any errors.

Another form of accounting that we all dread is the filing of annual federal income tax returns. Many people use a CPA to do their returns; others do it themselves. Most forms include the following items:

Income - any money you've earned from working or owning assets, unless there are specific exemptions from income tax.

Personal exemptions - this is a certain amount of income that is excused from tax.
Standard deduction - some personal expenditures or business expenses can be deducted from your income to reduce the taxable amount of income. These expenses include items such as interest paid on your home mortgage, charitable contributions and property taxes.
Taxable income - This is the balance of income that's subject to taxes after personal exemptions and deductions are factored in. More on personal finance in a bit.

Making a Profit

Accountants are responsible for preparing three primary types of financial statements for a business. The income statement reports the profit-making activities of the business and the bottom-line profit or loss for a specified period. The balance sheets reports the financial position of the business at a specific point in time, often the last day of the period. And the statement of cash flows reports how much cash was generated from profit what the business did with this money.

Everyone knows profit is a good thing. It's what our economy is founded on. It doesn't sound like such a big deal. Make more money than you spend to sell or manufacture products. But of course nothing's ever really simple, is it? A profit report, or net income statement first identifies the business and the time period that is being summarized in the report.

You read an income statement from the top line to the bottom line. Every step of the income statement reports the deduction of an expense. The income statement also reports changes in assets and liabilities as well, so that if there's a revenue increase, it's either because there's been an increase in assets or a decrease in a company's liabilities. If there's been an increase in the expense line, it's because there's been either a decrease in assets or an increase in liabilities.

Net worth is also referred to as owners' equity in the business. They're not exactly interchangeable. Net worth expresses the total of assets less the liabilities. Owners' equity refers to who owns the assets after the liabilities are satisfied.

These shifts in assets and liabilities are important to owners and executives of a business because it's their responsibility to manage and control such changes. Making a profit in a business involves several variable, not just increasing the amount of cash that flows through a company, but management of other assets as well.

Assets and Liabilities

Making a profit in a business is derived from several different areas. It can get a little complicated because just as in our personal lives, business is run on credit as well. Many businesses sell their products to their customers on credit. Accountants use an asset account called accounts receivable to record the total amount owed to the business by its customers who haven't paid the balance in full yet. Much of the time, a business hasn't collected its receivables in full by the end of the fiscal year, especially for such credit sales that could be transacted near the end of the accounting period.

The accountant records the sales revenue and the cost of goods sold for these sales in the year in which the sales were made and the products delivered to the customer. This is called accrual based accounting, which records revenue when sales are made and records expenses when they're incurred as well. When sales are made on credit, the accounts receivable asset account is increased. When cash is received from the customer, then the cash account is increased and the accounts receivable account is decreased.

The cost of goods sold is one of the major expenses of businesses that sell goods, products or services. Even a service involves expenses. It means exactly what it says in that it's the cost that a business pays for the products it sells to customers. A business makes its profit by selling its products at prices high enough to cover the cost of producing them, the costs of running the business, the interest on any money they've borrowed and income taxes, with money left over for profit.

When the business acquires products, the cost of them goes into what's called an inventory asset account. The cost is deducted from the cash account, or added to the accounts payable liability account, depending on whether the business has paid with cash or credit.

Gains and Losses

It would probably be ideal if business and life were as simple as producing goods, selling them and recording the profits. But there are often circumstances that disrupt the cycle, and it's part of the accountants job to report these as well. Changes in the business climate, or cost of goods or any number of things can lead to exceptional or extraordinary gains and losses in a business. Some things that can alter the income statement can include downsizing or restructuring the business. This used to be a rare thing in the business environment, but is now fairly commonplace. Usually it's done to offset losses in other areas and to decrease the cost of employees' salaries and benefits. However, there are costs involved with this as well, such as severance pay, outplacement services, and retirement costs.

In other circumstances, a business might decide to discontinue certain product lines. Western Union, for example, recently delivered its very last telegram. The nature of communication has changed so drastically, with email, cell phones and other forms, that telegrams have been rendered obsolete. When you no longer sell enough of a product at a high enough profit to make the costs of manufacturing it worthwhile, then it's time to change your product mix.

Lawsuits and other legal actions can cause extraordinary losses or gains as well. If you win damages in a lawsuit against others, then you've incurred an extraordinary gain. Likewise if your own legal fees and damages or fines are excessive, then these can significantly impact the income statement.

Occasionally a business will change accounting methods or need to correct any errors that had been made in previous financial reports. Generally Accepted Accounting Procedures (GAAP) require that businesses make any one-time losses or gains very visible in their income statement.

The Balance Sheet

A balance sheet is a quick picture of the financial condition of a business at a specific period in time. The activities of a business fall into two separate groups that are reported by an accountant. They are profit-making activities, which includes sales and expenses. This can also be referred to as operating activities. There are also financing and investing activities that include securing money from debt and equity sources of capital, returning capital to these sources, making distributions from profit to the owners, making investments in assets and eventually disposing of the assets.

Profit making activities are reported in the income statement; financing and investing activities are found in the statement of cash flows. In other words, two different financial statements are prepared for the two different types of transactions. The statement of cash flows also reports the cash increase or decrease from profit during the year as opposed to the amount of profit that is reported in the income statement.

The balance sheet is different from the income and cash flow statements which report, as it says, income of cash and outgoing cash. The balance sheet represents the balances, or amounts, or a company's assets, liabilities and owners' equity at an instant in time. The word balance has different meanings at different times. As it's used in the term balance sheet, it refers to the balance of the two opposite sides of a business, total assets on one side and total liabilities on the other. However, the balance of an account, such as the asset, liability, revenue and expense accounts, refers to the amount in the account after recording increases and decreases in the account, just like the balance in your checking account. Accountants can prepare a balance sheet any time that a manager requests it. But they're generally prepared at the end of each month, quarter and year. It's always prepared at the close of business on the last day of the profit period.

Revenue and Receivables

In most businesses, what drives the balance sheet are sales and expenses. In other words, they cause the assets and liabilities in a business. One of the more complicated accounting items are the accounts receivable. As a hypothetical situation, imagine a business that offers all its customers a 30-day credit period, which is fairly common in transactions between businesses, (not transactions between a business and individual consumers).

An accounts receivable asset shows how much money customers who bought products on credit still owe the business. It's a promise of case that the business will receive. Basically, accounts receivable is the amount of uncollected sales revenue at the end of the accounting period. Cash does not increase until the business actually collects this money from its business customers. However, the amount of money in accounts receivable is included in the total sales revenue for that same period. The business did make the sales, even if it hasn't acquired all the money from the sales yet. Sales revenue, then isn't equal to the amount of cash that the business accumulated.

To get actual cash flow, the accountant must subtract the amount of credit sales not collected from the sales revenue in cash. Then add in the amount of cash that was collected for the credit sales that were made in the preceding reporting period. If the amount of credit sales a business made during the reporting period is greater than what was collected from customers, then the accounts receivable account increased over the period and the business has to subtract from net income that difference.

If the amount they collected during the reporting period is greater than the credit sales made, then the accounts receivable decreased over the reporting period, and the accountant needs to add to net income that difference between the receivables at the beginning of the reporting period and the receivables at the end of the same period.

Inventory and Expenses

Inventory is usually the largest current asset of a business that sells products. If the inventory account is greater at the end of the period than at the start of the reporting period, the amount the business actually paid in cash for that inventory is more than what the business recorded as its cost of good sold expense. When that occurs, the accountant deducts the inventory increase from net income for determining cash flow from profit.

The prepaid expenses asset account works in much the same way as the change in inventory and accounts receivable accounts. However, changes in prepaid expenses are usually much smaller than changes in those other two asset accounts.

The beginning balance of prepaid expenses is charged to expense in the current year, but the cash was actually paid out last year. this period, the business pays cash for next period's prepaid expenses, which affects this period's cash flow, but doesn't affect net income until the next period. Simple, right?

As a business grows, it needs to increase its prepaid expenses for such things as fire insurance premiums, which have to be paid in advance of the insurance coverage, and its stocks of office supplies. Increases in accounts receivable, inventory and prepaid expenses are the cash flow price a business has to pay for growth. Rarely do you find a business that can increase its sales revenue without increasing these assets.

The lagging behind effect of cash flow is the price of business growth. Managers and investors need to understand that increasing sales without increasing accounts receivable isn't a realistic scenario for growth. In the real business world, you generally can't enjoy growth in revenue without incurring additional expenses.

Depreciation

Depreciation is a term we hear about frequently, but don't really understand. It's an essential component of accounting however. Depreciation is an expense that's recorded at the same time and in the same period as other accounts. Long-term operating assets that are not held for sale in the course of business are called fixed assets. Fixed assets include buildings, machinery, office equipment, vehicles, computers and other equipment. It can also include items such as shelves and cabinets. Depreciation refers to spreading out the cost of a fixed asset over the years of its useful life to a business, instead of charging the entire cost to expense in the year the asset was purchased. That way, each year that the equipment or asset is used bears a share of the total cost. As an example, cars and trucks are typically depreciated over five years. The idea is to charge a fraction of the total cost to depreciation expense during each of the five years, rather than just the first year.

Depreciation applies only to fixed assets that you actually buy, not those you rent or lease. Depreciation is a real expense, but not necessarily a cash outlay expense in the year it's recorded. The cash outlay does actually occur when the fixed asset is acquired, but is recorded over a period of time.

Depreciation is different from other expenses. It is deducted from sales revenue to determine profit, but the depreciation expense recorded in a reporting period doesn't require any true cash outlay during that period. Depreciation expense is that portion of the total cost of a business's fixed assets that is allocated to the period to record the cost of using the assets during period. The higher the total cost of a business's fixed assets, then the higher its depreciation expense.

Depreciation Reporting

In an accountant's reporting systems, depreciation of a business's fixed assets such as its buildings, equipment, computers, etc. is not recorded as a cash outlay. When an accountant measures profit on the accrual basis of accounting, he or she counts depreciation as an expense. Buildings, machinery, tools, vehicles and furniture all have a limited useful life. All fixed assets, except for actual land, have a limited lifetime of usefulness to a business. Depreciation is the method of accounting that allocates the total cost of fixed assets to each year of their use in helping the business generate revenue.

Part of the total sales revenue of a business includes recover of cost invested in its fixed assets. In a real sense a business sells some of its fixed assets in the sales prices that it charges it customers. For example, when you go to a grocery store, a small portion of the price you pay for eggs or bread goes toward the cost of the buildings, the machinery, bread ovens, etc. Each reporting period, a business recoups part of the cost invested in its fixed assets.

It's not enough for the accountant to add back depreciation for the year to bottom-line profit. The changes in other assets, as well as the changes in liabilities, also affect cash flow from profit. The competent accountant will factor in all the changes that determine cash flow from profit. Depreciation is only one of many adjustments to the net income of a business to determine cash flow from operating activities. Amortization of intangible assets is another expense that is recorded against a business's assets for year. It's different in that it doesn't require cash outlay in the year being charged with the expense. That occurred when the business invested in those tangible assets.

Investing and Financing

Another portion of the statement of cash flows reports the investment that the company took during the reporting year. New investments are signs of growing or upgrading the production and distribution facilities and capacity of the business. Disposing of long-term assets or divesting itself of a major part of its business can be good or bad news, depending on what's driving those activities. A business generally disposes of some of its fixed assets every year because they reached the end of their useful lives and will not be used any longer. These fixed assets are disposed of or sold or traded in on new fixed assets. The value of a fixed asset at the end of its useful life is called its salvage value. The proceeds from selling fixed assets are reported as a source of cash in the investing activities section of the statement of cash flows. Usually these are very small amounts.

Like individuals, companies at times have to finance its acquisitions when its internal cash flow isn't enough to finance business growth. Financing refers to a business raising capital from debt and equity sources, by borrowing money from banks and other sources willing to loan money to the business and by its owners putting additional money in the business. The term also includes the other side, making payments on debt and returning capital to owners. it includes cash distributions by the business from profit to its owners.

Most business borrow money for both short terms and long terms. Most cash flow statements report only the net increase or decrease in short-term debt, not the total amounts borrowed and total payments on the debt. When reporting long-term debt, however, both the total amounts and the repayments on long-term debt during a year are generally reported in the statement of cash flows. These are reported as gross figures, rather than net.

Building a Cash Cushion

Building a financial cushion for your business is never easy. Experts say that businesses should have anywhere from six to nine month's worth of income safely stored away in the bank. If you're a business grossing $250,000 per month, the mere thought of saving over $1.5 million dollars in a savings account will either have you collapsing from fits of laughter or from the paralyzing panic that has just set in. What may be a nice well-advised idea in theory can easily be tossed right out the window when you're just barely making payroll each month. So how is a small business owner to even begin a prudent savings program for long-term success?

Realizing that your business needs a savings plan is the first step toward better management. The reasons for growing a financial nest egg are strong. Building savings allows you to plan for future growth in your business and have ready the investment capital necessary to launch those plans. Having a source of back-up income can often carry a business through a rough time.

When market fluctuations, such as the dramatic increase in gasoline and oil prices, start to affect your business, you may need to dip into your savings to keep operations running smoothly until the difficulties pass. Savings can also support seasonal businesses with the ability to purchase inventory and cover payroll until the flush of new cash arrives. Try to remember that you didn't build your business overnight and you cannot build a savings account instantly either.

Review your books monthly and see where you can trim expenses and reroute the savings to a separate account. This will also help to keep you on track with cash flow and other financial issues. While it can be quite alarming to see your cash flowing outward with seemingly no end in sight, it's better to see it happening and put corrective measures into place, rather than discovering your losses five or six months too late.

Software Programs

Accounting has become more and more complex as have the businesses that use accounting functions. Fortunately, there are several excellent software packages that can help you manage this important function. Quasar is one such package.

All versions of Quasar offer comprehensive inventory controls. In its most basic use, the inventory module allows a business owner to track the locations and quantities of all inventory items. Additionally, the inventory capabilities go beyond simple record-keeping. Manufacturers and wholesalers can assemble kits using component items; whenever a kit is assembled, the inventory representing its component items are adjusted accordingly. Items can be grouped into various categories and the groups can be nested many levels deep. Vendor purchase orders can be generated for items whose quantities are below a preset level. Costs and selling prices for items can be set and discounted in a myriad of different ways. Finally, these items can be reported upon to show such things as profits, margins, and sales per item.

Sales and purchasing are another strength of Quasar. Customer quotes can be easily converted to invoices to be paid. Promotions can be created and discounts can be given based on date, customer, or store location. Margins can be reported upon for traits such as individual items, individual customers, or individual salesperson. Likewise, a purchase order can be created and converted to a vendor invoice, which can be paid in a number of different ways, including printing a check. Quasar can keep track of miscellaneous fees such as container deposits, freight charges, and franchise fees.

The intelligent design of Quasar's user interface allows for quick and easy data entry. Some programs you may encounter are not optimized for keyboard use. These programs require you to move your hand to the mouse to select frequently needed options. While some of Quasar's menu options are only mouse-accessible, the bulk of Quasar's user interface is designed in such a way that you can keep you hands on the keyboard by using special shortcuts. This allows for faster data entry, which can save time (and therefore money) in the long run.

Perhaps the software most used and suited to small businesses is **Intuit's Quickbooks**. The simple and extremely affordable plans can allow a small business to effectively manage their accounting needs. You can create estimates and send invoices, download all bank transactions, accept credit cards, manage and pay bills, prepare 1099's for contractors, and make use of their online payroll and file payroll withholding taxes. Intuit really makes a complicated subject simple for you.
FREE 30 Day Trial to Intuit's Quickbooks.
 http://quickbooks.intuit.com/signup

For an automated bookkeeping system that works like mint.com, use **www.outright.com**. It is simple and pulls in your transactions and categorizes them for you without having to do it manually. At $10 a month or so, it is worth it. And it can help you gather what you need at the year end or quarterly for tax purposes.

Buy the Best Accounting Software

You may want a more robust option. One of the most important decisions that you will have to make while starting or operating your small business is that of which accounting software to use. It could certainly be a nightmare if you make the wrong choice.

During the past 20 years accounting software has advanced far beyond the old fashioned basic lined accounting books with 'in' and 'out' columns. Nowadays it is wholly possible to find accounting software that will assist you in all of your personal and business accounting tasks, from accounts receivable to online banking. With such a wide array of accounting software packages available, It can be difficult to decide which accounting software program will best fit your needs.

Before choosing an accounting software program it is worth while that you give some thought to exactly why you desire the program in the first place. There is really or no point in buying a software program that enables you to keep track of accounts receivable and issued invoices if you just need the software to do your home budgeting. On the other hand, if you are a small to medium business, then it's quite likely that the ability to manage your issued and outstanding invoices is essential.

It would be wise to investigate the type of support you get when you purchase accounting software. A good support plan would include at least 30 days free support upon registration. You should be able to easily find answers to commonly asked questions or ask a question specific to your support needs and get accurate online answers quickly.

The form in which the accounting software package is going to interact with your other software is another factor that you need to consider. For example, if you make use of online banking, then a very useful feature would be the ability of the software package to update with your online bank statements. Furthermore, if you possess a number of different income streams, and you find it necessary to be sure that all of them are being included in your budget, then software that allows you to take advantage of this facility may be beneficial. However, if all you have is one or two income streams and all you want to do is keep a track on what your household outgoing expenditures are, then you might just need a simple Excel accounting software package.

Finally, before making a selection on any particular accounting software package, it would be best to make sure your computer has the correct system requirements for the application. For example, you should make sure you have enough room on your hard-drive to download the program and that you don't already have the applicable software on your system. Bear in mind that there is nothing more frustrating than acquiring a new software package only to find out that it's not compatible with your computer setup.

You can probably see that the issue of choosing the best accounting software is not a simple one. All in all probably the most important factor is ease of use, since you're going to have to work with the software nearly every day if you own a small business.

Managing the Bottom Line

If you don't keep track of how much money you're making, you have no idea whether your business is successful or not. You can't tell how well your marketing is working. And I don't just mean you should know the amount of your total sales or gross revenue. You need to know what your net profit is. If you don't, there's no way you can know how to increase it.

If you want your business to be successful, you need to make a financial plan and check it against the facts on a monthly basis, then take immediate action to correct any problems. Here are the steps you should take:

* Create a financial plan for your business. Estimate how much revenue you expect to bring in each month, and project what your expenses will be.

* Remember that lost profits can't be recovered. When entrepreneurs compare their projections to reality and find earnings too low or expenses too high, they often conclude, "I'll make it up later." The problem is that you really can't make it up later: every month profits are too low is a month that is gone forever.

* Make adjustments right away. If revenues are lower than expected, increase efforts in sales and marketing or look for ways to increase your rates. If overhead costs are too high, find ways to cut back. There are other businesses like yours around. What is their secret for operating profitably?
* Think before you spend. When considering any new business expense, including marketing and sales activities, evaluate the increased earnings you expect to bring in against its cost before you proceed to make a purchase.

* Evaluate the success of your business based on profit, not revenue. It doesn't matter how many thousands of dollars you are bringing in each month if your expenses are almost as high, or higher. Many high-revenue businesses have gone under for this very reason -- don't be one of them.

What is the FASB?

The FASB is one organization that provides standardized guidelines for financial reporting. The mission of the Financial Accounting Standards Board (FASB) is to establish and improve standards of financial accounting and reporting for the guidance and education of the public, including issuers, auditors and users of financial information.

Accounting standards are essential to the efficient functioning of the economy because decisions about the allocation of resources rely heavily on credible, concise, transparent and understandable financial information. Financial information about the operations and financial position of individual entities also is used by the public in making various other kinds of decisions.

To accomplish its mission, the FASB acts to:
--Improve the usefulness of financial reporting by focusing on the primary characteristics of relevance and reliability and on the qualities of comparability and consistency;

--Keep standards current to reflect changes in methods of doing business and changes in the economic environment;

--Consider promptly any significant areas of deficiency in financial reporting that might be improved through the standard-setting process;

--Promote the international convergence of accounting standards concurrent with improving the quality of financial reporting; and

--Improve the common understanding of the nature and purposes of information contained in financial reports.

The FASB develops broad accounting concepts as well as standards for financial reporting. It also provides guidance on implementation of standards. Concepts are useful in guiding the Board in establishing standards and in providing a frame of reference, or conceptual framework, for resolving accounting issues. The framework will help to establish reasonable bounds for judgment in preparing financial information and to increase understanding of, and confidence in, financial information on the part of users of financial reports. It also will help the public to understand the nature and limitations of information supplied by financial reporting.

What are Auditors?

Accountants and auditors help to ensure that the Nation's firms are run efficiently, its public records kept accurately, and its taxes paid properly and on time. They perform these vital functions by offering an increasingly wide array of business and accounting services, including public, management, and government accounting, as well as internal auditing, to their clients. Beyond carrying out the fundamental tasks of the occupation- preparing, analyzing, and verifying financial documents in order to provide information to clients-many accountants now are required to possess a wide range of knowledge and skills. Accountants and auditors are broadening the services they offer to include budget analysis, financial and investment planning, information technology consulting, and limited legal services.

Specific job duties vary widely among the four major fields of accounting: public, management, and government accounting and internal auditing.

Internal auditors verify the accuracy of their organization's internal records and check for mismanagement, waste, or fraud. Internal auditing is an increasingly important area of accounting and auditing. Internal auditors examine and evaluate their firms' financial and information systems, management procedures, and internal controls to ensure that records are accurate and controls are adequate to protect against fraud and waste. They also review company operations, evaluating their efficiency, effectiveness, and compliance with corporate policies and procedures, laws, and government regulations. There are many types of highly specialized auditors, such as electronic data-processing, environmental, engineering, legal, insurance premium, bank, and health care auditors. As computer systems make information timelier, internal auditors help managers to base their decisions on actual data, rather than personal observation. Internal auditors also may recommend controls for their organization's computer system, to ensure the reliability of the system and the integrity of the data.

Government accountants and auditors work in the public sector, maintaining and examining the records of government agencies and auditing private businesses and individuals whose activities are subject to government regulations or taxation. Accountants employed by Federal, State, and local governments guarantee that revenues are received and expenditures are made in accordance with laws and regulations. Those employed by the Federal Government may work as Internal Revenue Service agents or in financial management, financial institution examination, or budget analysis and administration.

What is Forensic Accounting?

Forensic accounting is the practice of utilizing accounting, auditing, and investigative skills to assist in legal matters. It encompasses 2 main areas - litigation support, investigation, and dispute resolution. Litigation support represents the factual presentation of economic issues related to existing or pending litigation. In this capacity, the forensic accounting professional quantifies damages sustained by parties involved in legal disputes and can assist in resolving disputes, even before they reach the courtroom. If a dispute reaches the courtroom, the forensic accountant may testify as an expert witness.

Investigation is the act of determining whether criminal matters such as employee theft, securities fraud (including falsification of financial statements), identity theft, and insurance fraud have occurred. As part of the forensic accountant's work, he or she may recommend actions that can be taken to minimize future risk of loss. Investigation may also occur in civil matters. For example, the forensic accountant may search for hidden assets in divorce cases.

Forensic accounting involves looking beyond the numbers and grasping the substance of situations. It's more than accounting...more than detective work...it's a combination that will be in demand for as long as human nature exists. Who wouldn't want a career that offers such stability, excitement, and financial rewards?

In short, forensic accounting requires the most important quality a person can possess: the ability to think. Far from being an ability that is specific to success in any particular field, developing the ability to think enhances a person's chances of success in life, thus increasing a person's worth in today's society.   Why not consider becoming a forensic accountant on the Forensic Accounting Masters Degree link on the left-hand navigation bar.

Who Uses Forensic Accountants?

Forensic accounting financial investigative specialists work with financial information for the purpose of conveying complicated issues in a manner that others can easily understand.   While some forensic accountants and forensic accounting specialists are engaged in the public practice of forensic examination, others work in private industry for such entities as banks and insurance companies or governmental entities such as sheriff and police departments, the Federal Bureau of Investigation (FBI), and the Internal Revenue Service (IRS).

The occupational fraud committed by employees usually involves the theft of assets. Embezzlement has been the most often committed fraud for the last 30 years. Employees may be involved in kickback schemes, identity theft, or conversion of corporate assets for personal use. The forensic accountant couples observation of the suspected employees with physical examination of assets, invigilation, inspection of documents, and interviews of those involved. Experience on these types of engagements enables the forensic accountant to offer suggestions as to internal controls that owners could implement to reduce the likelihood of fraud.

At times, the forensic accountant may be hired by attorneys to investigate the financial trail of persons suspected of engaging in criminal activity. Information provided by the forensic accountant may be the most effective way of obtaining convictions. The forensic accountant may also be engaged by bankruptcy court when submitted financial information is suspect or if employees (including managers) are suspected of taking assets.

Opportunities for qualified forensic accounting professionals abound in private companies. CEOs must now certify that their financial statements are faithful representations of the financial position and results of operations of their companies and rely more heavily on internal controls to detect any misstatement that would otherwise be contained in these financials.

In addition to these activities, forensic accountants may be asked to determine the amount of the loss sustained by victims, testify in court as an expert witness and assist in the preparation of visual aids and written summaries for use in court.

What is the Sarbanes-Oxley Act?

The Sarbanes-Oxley Act of 2002 is a United States federal law passed in response to the recent major corporate and accounting scandals including those at Enron, Tyco International, and WorldCom (now MCI). These scandals resulted in a decline of public trust in accounting and reporting practices. Named after sponsors Senator Paul Sarbanes (D-Md.) and Representative Michael G. Oxley (R-Oh.), the Act was approved by the House by a vote of 423-3 and by the Senate 99-0. The legislation is wide-ranging and establishes new or enhanced standards for all U.S. public company Boards, Management, and public accounting firms. The first and most important part of the Act establishes a new quasi-public agency, the Public Company Accounting Oversight Board, which is charged with overseeing and disciplining accounting firms in their roles as auditors of public companies. Some of the major provisions of the Sarbanes-Oxley Act's include:

--Certification of financial reports by chief executive officers and chief financial officers

--Auditor independence, including outright bans on certain types of work for audit clients and pre-certification by the company's Audit Committee of all other non-audit work

--A requirement that companies listed on stock exchanges have fully independent audit committees that oversee the relationship between the company and its auditor

--Significantly longer maximum jail sentences and larger fines for corporate executives who knowingly and willfully misstate financial statements, although maximum sentences are largely irrelevant because judges generally follow the Federal Sentencing Guidelines in setting actual sentences

--Employee protections allowing those corporate fraud whistleblowers who file complaints with OSHA within 90 days, to win reinstatement, back pay and benefits, compensatory damages, abatement orders, and reasonable attorney fees and costs.

Disclosure
Financial statements are the backbone of a complete financial report. In fact, a financial report is not complete if the three primary financial statements are not included. but a financial report is much more than just those statements. A financial report requires disclosures. This term refers to additional information provided in a financial report. Therefore, any comprehensive and ethical financial report must include not only the primary financial statements, but disclosures as well.

The chief executive of a business (usually the CEO in a publicly held corporation) has the primary responsibility to make sure that the financial statements have been prepared according to generally accepted accounting principles (GAAP) and the financial report provides adequate disclosures. He or she works with the chief financial officer or controller of the business to make sure that the financial report meets the standard of adequate disclosures.

Some common methods of disclosures include:
--Footnotes that provide information about the basic figures. Nearly all financial statements require footnotes to provide additional information for several of the account balances in the financial statements.

--Supplementary financial schedules and tables that provide more details than can be included in the body of the financial statements.

--Other information may be required if the business is a public corporation subject to federal regulations regarding financial reporting to its stockholders. Other information is voluntary and not strictly required legally or according to GAAP.

Some disclosures are required by various governing boards and agencies. These include:

--The financial Accounting Standards Board (FASB) has designated many standards. Its dictate regarding disclosure of the effects of stock options is one such standard.

--The Securities and Exchange Commission (SEC) mandates disclosure of a broad range of information for publicly held companies.

--International businesses have to abide by disclosure standards adopted by the International Accounting Standards Board.

What is Financial Window Dressing

Financial managers can do certain things to increase or decrease net income that's recorded in the year. This is called profit smoothing, income smoothing or just plain old window dressing. This isn't the same as fraud, or cooking the books.

Most profit smoothing involves pushing some amount of revenue and/or expenses into other years than they would normally be recorded. A common technique for profit smoothing is to delay normal maintenance and repairs. This is referred to as deferred maintenance. Many routine and recurring maintenance costs required for autos, trucks, machines, equipment and buildings can be delayed, or deferred until later.

A business that spends a significant amount of money for employee training and development may delay these programs until the next year so the expense in the current year is lower.

A company can cut back on its current year's outlays for market research and product development.

A business can ease up on its rules regarding when slow-paying customers are written off to expense as bad debts or uncollectible accounts receivable. The business can put off recording some of its bad debts expense until the next reporting year.

A fixed asset that is not being actively used may have very little current or future value to a business. Instead of writing off the un-depreciated cost of the impaired asset as a loss in the current year, the business might delay the write-off until the next year.

You can see how manipulating the timing of certain expenses can make an impact on net income. This isn't illegal although companies can go too far in massaging the numbers so that its financial statements are misleading. For the most part though, profit smoothing isn't much more than robbing Peter to pay Paul. Accountants refer to these as compensatory effects. The effects next year offset and cancel out the effects in the current year. Less expense this year is balanced by more expense the next year.

What is a Corporation?

Most businesses start out as a small company, owned by one person or by a partnership. The most common type of business when there are multiple owners is a corporation. The law sees a corporation as real, live person. Like an adult, a corporation is treated as a distinct and independent individual who has rights and responsibilities. A corporation's "birth certificate" is the legal form that is filed with the Secretary of State of the state in which the corporation is created, or incorporated. It must have a legal name, just like a person.

A corporation is separate from its owners. It's responsible for its own debts. The bank can't come after the stockholders if a corporation goes bankrupt.

A corporation issues ownership share to persons who invest money in the business. These ownership shares are documented by stock certificates, which state the name of the owner and how many shares are owned. the corporation has to keep a register, or list, of how many shares everyone owns. Owners of a corporation are called stockholders because they own shares of stock issued by the corporation. One share of stock is one unit of ownership; how much one share is worth depends on the total number of shares that the business issues. the more shares a business issues, the smaller the percentage of total owners' equity each share represents.

Stock shares come in different classes of stock. Preferred stockholders are promised a certain amount of cash dividends each year. Common stockholders have the most risk. If a corporation ends up in financial trouble, it's required to pay off its liabilities first. If any money is left over, then that money goes first to the preferred stockholders. If anything is left over after that, then that money is distributed to the common stockholders.

What are Partnerships and Limited Liability Companies?

Some business owners choose to create partnerships or limited liability companies instead of a corporation. A partnership can also be called a firm, and refers to an association of a group of individuals working together in a business or professional practice.

While corporations have rigid rules about how they are structured, partnerships and limited liability companies allow the division of management authority, profit sharing and ownership rights among the owners to be very flexible.

Partnerships fall into two categories. General partners are subject to unlimited liability. If a business can't pay its debts, its creditors can demand payment from the general partners' personal assets. General partners have the authority and responsibility to manage the business. They're analogous to the president and other officers of a corporation.

Limited partners escape the unlimited liability that the general partners have. They are not responsible as individuals, for the liabilities of the partnership. These are junior partners who have ownership rights to the profits of the business, but they don't generally participate in the high-level management of the business. A partnership must have one or more general partners.

A limited liability company (LLC) is becoming more prevalent among smaller businesses. An LLC is like a corporation regarding limited liability and it's like a partnership regarding the flexibility of dividing profit among the owners. Its advantage over other types of ownership is its flexibility in how profit and management authority are determined. This can have a downside. The owners must enter into very detailed agreements about how the profits and management responsibilities are divided. It can get very complicated and generally requires the services of a lawyer to draw up the agreement.

A partnership or LLC agreement specifies how profits will be divided among the owners. While stockholders of a corporation receive a share of profit that's directly related to how many shares they own, a partnership or LLC does not have to divide profit according to how much each partner invested. Invested capital is only of the factors that are used in allocating and distributing profits.

What is a Sole Proprietorship?

A sole proprietorship is the business or an individual who has decided not to carry his business as a separate legal entity, such as a corporation, partnership or limited liability company. This kind of business is not a separate entity. Any time a person regularly provides services for a fee, sells things at a flea market or engage in any business activity whose primary purpose is to make a profit, that person is a sole proprietor. If they carry on business activity to make profit or income, the IRS requires that you file a separate Schedule C "Profit or Loss From a Business" with your annual individual income tax return. Schedule C summarizes your income and expenses from your sole proprietorship business.

As the sole proprietor of a business, you have unlimited liability, meaning that if your business can't pay all it liabilities, the creditors to whom your business owes money can come after your personal assets. Many part-time entrepreneurs may not know this, but it's an enormous financial risk. If they are sued or can't pay their bills, they are personally liable for the business's liabilities.

A sole proprietorship has no other owners to prepare financial statements for, but the proprietor should still prepare these statements to know how his business is doing. Banks usually require financial statements from sole proprietors who apply for loans. A partnership needs to maintain a separate capital or ownership account for each partners. The total profit of the firm is allocated into these capital accounts, as spelled out in the partnership agreement. Although sole proprietors don't have separate invested capital from retained earnings like corporations do, they still need to keep these two separate accounts for owners' equity - not only to track the business, but for the benefit of any future buyers of the business.

Budgeting

Ugh, budgeting is one of those topics we'd rather avoid, but in business, it's an absolute necessity. To prepare a reasoned and thoughtful budget, an accountant must start with a broad-based critical analysis of the most recent actual performance and position of the business by the managers who are responsible for the results. Then the managers decide on specific and concrete goals for the coming year. It demands a fair amount of management time and energy. Budgets should be worth this time and effort. It's one of the key components of a manager's job.

To construct budgeted financial statements, a manager needs good models of the profit, cash flow and financial condition of your business. Models are blueprints or schematics of how things work. A business budget is, at its core, a financial blueprint of the business. Budgeting relies on financial models that are the foundation for preparing budgeted financial statements. Those statements include:

--Budgeted income statement (or profit report): This statement highlights the critical information that managers need for making decisions and exercising control. Much of the information in an internal profit report is confidential and should not be divulged outside the business.

--Budgeted balance sheet: The connections and ratios between sales revenue and expenses and their corresponding assets and liabilities are the elements of the basic model for the budgeted balance sheet.

--Budgeted statement of cash flows: The changes in assets and liabilities from their balances at the end of the year just concluded to the projected balances at the end of the coming year determine cash flow from profit for the coming year.

Budgeting requires good working models of profit performance, financial condition, and cash flow from profit. Constructing good budgets is a strong incentive for businesses to develop financial models that not only help in the budgeting process but also help managers in making strategic decisions.

About GAAP

While many businesses assume that accountants are bound by generally accepted accounting practices and that these are inviolate, nothing could be further from the truth. Everything is subject to interpretation, and GAAP is no different. For one thing, GAAP themselves permit alternative accounting methods to be used for certain expenses and for revenue in certain specialized types of businesses. For another, GAAP methods require that decisions be made about the timing for recording revenue and expenses, or they require that key factors be quantified. Deciding on the timing of revenue and expenses and putting definite values on these factors require judgments, estimates and interpretations.

The mission of GAAP over the years has been to standardize accounting methods in order to bring about uniformity across all businesses. But alternative methods are still permitted for certain basic business expenses. No tests are required to determine whether one method is more preferable than another. A business is free to select whichever method it wants. But it must choose which cost of good sold expense method to use and which depreciation expense method to use.

For other expenses and for sales revenue, one general accounting method has been established; there are no alternative methods. However, a business has a fair amount of latitude in actually implementing the methods. One business applies the accounting methods in a conservative manner, and another business applies the methods in a more liberal manner. The end result is more diversity between businesses in their profit measure and financial statements than one might expect, considering that GAAP have been evolving since 1930.

The pronouncement on GAAP prepared by the Financial Accounting Standards Board (FASB) is now more than 1000 pages long. And that doesn't even include the rules and regulations issued by the federal regulatory agency that jurisdiction over the financial reporting and accounting methods of publicly owned businesses - the Securities and Exchange Commission (SEC).

Types of Costs

Direct costs are those costs that can be directly attributed to a product or product line, or to one source of sales revenue, or one business unit or operation of the business. An example of a direct cost would be the cost of tires on a new automobile.

Indirect costs are very different and can't be attached to any specific product, unit or activity. The cost of labor or benefits for an auto manufacturer is certainly a cost, but it can't be attached to any one vehicle. Each business has to devise a method of allocating indirect costs to different products, sources of sales revenue, business units, etc. Most allocation methods are less than perfect, and generally end up being arbitrary to one degree or another. Business managers and accounts should always keep an eye on the allocation methods used for indirect costs and take the cost figures produced by these methods with a grain of salt.

Fixed costs are those costs that stay the same over a relatively broad range of sales volume or production output. They're like an albatross around the neck of business and a company must sell its product at a high enough price to at least break even.

Variable costs can increase and decrease in proportion to changes in sales or production level. Variable costs vary proportionately with changes in production.

Relevant costs are essentially future costs that could be incurred, depending on what strategic course a business takes. If an auto manufacturer decides to increase production, but the cost of tires goes up, than that cost needs to be taken into consideration.

Measuring Costs

Measuring profits or net income is the most important thing accountants do. The second most important task is measuring costs. Costs are extremely important to running a business and managing them effectively can make a substantial difference in a company's bottom line.

Any business that sells products needs to know its product costs and depending on what is being manufactured and/or sold, it can get complicated. Every step in the production process has to be tracked carefully from start to finish. Many manufacturing costs cannot be directly matched with particular products; these are called indirect costs. To calculate the full cost of each product manufactured, accountants devise methods for allocating indirect production costs to specific products. Generally accepted accounting principles (GAAP) provide few guidelines for measuring product cost.

Accountants need to determine many other costs, in addition to product costs, such as the costs of the departments and other organizational units of the business; the cost of the retirement plan for the company's employees; the cost of marketing and advertising; the cost of restructuring the business or the cost of a major recall of products sold by the company, should that ever become necessary.

Cost accounting serves two broad purposes: measuring profit and furnishing relevant information to managers. What makes it confusing is that there's no one set method for measuring and reporting costs, although accuracy is paramount. Cost accounting can fall anywhere on a continuum between conservative or expansive. The phrase actual cost depends entirely on the particular methods used to measure cost. These can often be as subjective and nebulous as some systems for judging sports. Again accuracy is extremely important. The total cost of goods or products sold is the first and usually largest expense deducted from sales revenue in measuring profit.

Parts of an Income Statement Part 1

The first and most important part of an income statement is the line reporting sales revenue. Businesses need to be consistent from year to year regarding when they record sales. For some business, the timing of recording sales revenue is a major problem, especially when the final acceptance by the customer depends on performance tests or other conditions that have to be satisfied. For example, when does an ad agency report the sales revenue for a campaign it's prepared for its client? When the work is completed and sent to the client for approval? When the client approves it? When the ads appear in the media? Or when the billing is complete? These are issues a company must decide on for reporting sales revenue, and they must be consistent each year, and the timing of reporting should be noted on the financial statement.

The next line in an income statement is the cost of goods sold expense. There are three methods of reporting cost of goods sold expense. One is called "first in-first out" (FIFO); another is the "last in-last out" (LIFO) method and the last is the average cost method. Cost of goods sold expense is a huge item in an income statement and how it's reported can make a substantial impact on the reported bottom line.

Other items in an income statement include inventory write-downs. A business should regularly inspect its inventory carefully to determine any losses due to theft, damage and deterioration, and to apply the lower of cost or market (LCM) method. Bad debts are also an important component of the income statement. Bad debts are those owed to a business by customers who bought on credit (accounts receivable) but are not going to be paid. Again the timing of when bad debts are reported is crucial. Do you report it before or after any collection efforts are exhausted?

Parts of an Income Statement Part 2

Of course profit and cost of goods sold expense are the two most critical components of an income statement, or at least they're what people will look at first. But an income statement is truly the sum of its parts, and they all need to be considered carefully, consistently and accurately.

In reporting depreciation expense, a business can use a short-life method and load most of the expense over the first few years, or a longer-life method and spread the expense evenly over the years. Depreciation is a big expense for some businesses and the method of reporting is especially critical for them.

One of the more complex elements of a an income statement is the line reporting employee pensions and post-retirement benefits. The GAAP rule on this expense is complex and several key estimates must be made by the business, such as the expected rate of return on the portfolio of funds set aside for these future obligations. This and other estimates affect the amount of expense recorded.

Many products are sold with expressed or implied warranties and guarantees. The business should estimate the cost of these future obligations and record this amount as an expense in the same period that the goods are sold, along with the cost of goods expense. It can't really wait until customers actually return products for repair or replacement, should be forecast as a percent of the total products sold.

Other operating expenses that are reported in an income statement may also have timing or estimating considerations. Some expenses are also discretionary in nature, which means that how much is spent during the year depends on the discretion of management.

Earnings before interest and tax (EBIT) measures the sales revenue less all the expenses above this line. It depends on all the decisions made for recording sales revenue and expenses and how the accounting methods are implemented.

Parts of an Income Statement Part 3

While some lines of an income statement depend on estimates or forecasts, the interest expense line is a basic equation. When accounting for income tax expense, however, a business can use different accounting methods for some of its expenses than it uses for calculating its taxable income. The hypothetical amount of taxable income, if the accounting methods used were used in the tax return is calculated. Then the income tax based on this hypothetical taxable income is fitured. This is the income tax expense reported in the income statement. This amount is reconciled with the actual amount of income tax owed based on the accounting methods used for income tax purposes. A reconciliation of the two different income tax amounts is then provided in a footnote on the income statement.

Net income is like earnings before interest and tax (EBIT) and can vary considerably depending on which accounting methods are used to report sales revenue and expenses. This is where profit smoothing can come into play to manipulate earnings. Profit smoothing crosses the line from choosing acceptable accounting methods from the list of GAAP and implementing these methods in a reasonable manner, into the gray area of earnings management that involves accounting manipulation.

It's incumbent on managers and business owners to be involved in the decisions about which accounting methods are used to measure profit and how those methods are actually implemented. A manager can be requires to answer questions about the company's financial reports on many occasions. It's therefore critical that any officer or manager in a company be thoroughly familiar with how the company's financial statements are prepared. Accounting methods and how they're implemented vary from business to business. A company's methods can fall anywhere on a continuum that's either left or right of center of GAAP.

How to Analyze a Financial Statement

It's obvious financial statements have a lot of numbers in them and at first glance it can seem unwieldy to read and understand. One way to interpret a financial report is to compute ratios, which means, divide a particular number in the financial report by another. Financial statement ratios are also useful because they enable the reader to compare a business's current performance with its past performance or with another business's performance, regardless of whether sales revenue or net income was bigger or smaller for the other years or the other business. In order words, using ratios can cancel out difference in company sizes.

There aren't many ratios in financial reports. Publicly owned businesses are required to report just one ratio (earnings per share, or EPS) and privately-owned businesses generally don't report any ratios. Generally accepted accounting principles (GAAP) don't require that any ratios be reported, except EPS for publicly owned companies.

Ratios don't provide definitive answers, however. They're useful indicators, but aren't the only factor in gauging the profitability and effectiveness of a company.

One ratio that's a useful indicator of a company's profitability is the gross margin ratio. This is the gross margin divided by the sales revenue. Businesses don't disclose margin information in their external financial reports. This information is considered to be proprietary in nature and is kept confidential to shield it from competitors.

The profit ratio is very important in analyzing the bottom-line of a company. It indicates how much net income was earned on each $100 of sales revenue. A profit ratio of 5 to 10 percent is common in most industries, although some highly price-competitive industries, such as retailers or grocery stores will show profit ratios of only one to two percent.

Earnings per Share

Publicly owned companies must report earnings per share (EPS) below the net income line in their income statements. This is mandated by generally accepted accounting practices (GAAP). The EPS gives investors a means of determining the amount the business earned on its stock share investments. In other words, EPS tells investors how much net income the business earned for each stock share they own. It's calculated by dividing net income by the total number of capital stock share. It's important to the stockholders who want the net income of the business to be communicated to them on a per share basis so they can compare it with the market price of their shares.

Private businesses don't have to report EPS because stockholders focus more on the business's total net income.

Publicly-held companies actually report two EPS figures, unless they have what's known as a simple capital structure. Most publicly-held companies though, have complex capital structures and have to report two EPS figures. One is called the basic EPS; the other is called the diluted EPS. Basic EPS is based on the number of stock shares that are outstanding. Diluted earnings are based on shares that are outstanding and shares that may be issued in the future in the form of stock options.

Obviously this is a complicated process. An accountant has to adjust the EPS formula for any number of occurrences or changes in the business. A business might issue additional stock shares during the year and buy back some of its own shares. Or it might issue several classes of stock, which will cause net income to be divided into two or more pools - one pool for each class of stock. A merger, acquisition or divestiture will also impact the formula for EPS.

What is Price/Earnings Ratio

The price/earnings (P/E) ratio is another measurement that's of particular interest to investors in public businesses. The P/E ratio gives you an idea of how much you're paying in the current price for stock shares for each dollar of earnings. Earnings prop up the market value of stock shares, not the book value of the stock shares that's reported in the balance sheet.

The P/E ratio is a reality check on just how high the current market price is in relation to the underlying profit that the business is earning. Extraordinarily high P/E ratios are justified only when investors think that the company's earnings per share (EPS) has a lot of upside potential in the future.

The P/E ratio is calculated dividing the current market price of the stock by the most recent trailing 12 months diluted EPS. Stock share prices bounce around day to day and are subject to big changes on short notice. The current P/E ratio should be compared with the average stock market P/E to gauge whether the business selling above or below the market average.

P/E ratios are currently running high, despite a four-year slump in the stock market. P/E ratios vary from industry to industry and from year to year. One dollar of EPS may command only a $10 market value for a mature business in a no-growth industry, while a dollar of EPS in a dynamic business in a growth industry may have a $30 market value per dollar of earnings, or net income.

To sum up, the price/earnings ratio, or P/E ratio is the current market price of a capital stock divided by its trailing 12 months' diluted earnings per share (EPS) or its basic earnings per share if the business does not report diluted EPS. A low P/E may signal an undervalued stock or a pessimistic forecast by investors. A high P/E may reveal an overvalued stock or might be based on an optimistic forecast by investors.

What's the Difference between Private and Public Company Reporting

A public corporation is a business whose securities are traded on the public stock exchanges, such as the New York Stock Exchange and Nasdaq. A private company is held solely by its owners and is not traded publicly. When the shareholders of a private business receive the periodical financial reports, they are entitled to assume that the company's financial statements and footnotes are prepared in accordance with GAAP. Otherwise the president of chief officer of the business should clearly warn the shareholders that GAAP have not been followed in one or more respects. The content of a private business's annual financial report is often minimal. It includes the three primary financial statements - the balance sheet, income statement and statement of cash flows. There's generally no letter from the chief executive, no photographs, no charts.

In contrast, the annual report of a publicly traded company has more bells and whistles to it. There are also more requirements for reporting. These include the management discussion and analysis (MD&A) section that presents the top managers' interpretation and analysis of the business's profit performance and other important financial developments over the year.

Another section required for public companies is the earnings per share (EPS). This is the only ratio that a public business is required to report, although most public companies report a few others as well. A three-year comparative income statement is also required.

Many publicly owned businesses make their required filings with the SEC, but they present very different annual financial reports to their stockholders. A large number of public companies include only condensed financial information rather than comprehensive financial statements. They will generally refer the reader to a more detailed SEC financial report for more specifics.

What are Other Ratios Used in Financial Reporting?

The dividend yield ratio tells investors how much cash income they're receiving on their stock investment in a business. This is calculated by dividing the annual cash dividend per share by the current market price of the stock. This can be compared with the interest rate on high-grade debt securities that pay interest, such as Treasure bonds and Treasury notes, which are the safest.

Book value per share is calculated by dividing total owners' equity by the total number of stock shares that are outstanding. While EPS is more important to determine the market value of a stock, book value per share is the measure of the recorded value of the company's assets less its liabilities, the net assets backing up the business's stock shares. It's possible that the market value of a stock could be less than the book value per share.

The return on equity (ROE) ratio tells how much profit a bus8iness earned in comparison to the book value of its stockholders' equity. This ratio is especially useful for privately owned businesses, which have no way of determining the current value of owners' equity. ROE is also calculated for public corporations, but it plays a secondary role to other ratios. ROE is calculated by dividing net income by owners' equity.

The current ratio is a measure of a business's short-term solvency, in other words, its ability to pay it liabilities that come due in the near future. This ratio is a rough indicator of whether cash on hand plus the cash to be collected from accounts receivable and from selling inventory will be enough to pay off the liabilities that will come due in the next period. It is calculated by dividing the current assets by the current liabilities. Businesses are expected to maintain a minimum 2:1 current ratio, which means its current assets should be twice its current liabilities.

What is Acid Test Ratio and ROA Ratio?

Investors calculate the acid test ratio, also known as the quick ratio or the pounce ratio. This ratio excludes inventory and prepaid expenses, which the current ratio includes, and it limits assets to cash and items that the business can quickly convert to cash. This limited category of assets is known as quick or liquid assets. The acid-text ratio is calculated by dividing the liquid assets by the total current liabilities.

This ratio is also known as the pounce ratio to emphasize that you're calculating for a worst-case scenario, where the business's creditors could pounce on the business and demand quick payment of the business's liabilities. Short term creditors do not have the right to demand immediate payment, except in unusual circumstances. This ratio is a conservative way to look at a business's capability to pay its short-term liabilities.

One factor that affects the bottom-line profitability of a business is whether it uses debt to its advantage. A business may realize a financial leverage gain, meaning it earns more profit on the money it has borrowed than the interest paid for the use of the borrowed money. A good part of a business's net income for the year may be due to financial leverage. The ROA ratio is determined by dividing the earnings before interest and income tax (EBIT) by the net operating assets.

An investor compares the ROA with the interest rate at which the corporation borrowed money. If a business's ROA is 14 percent and the interest rate on its debt is 8 percent, the business's net gain on its capital is 6 percent more than what it's paying in interest. ROA is a useful ratio for interpreting profit performance, aside from determining financial gain or loss. ROA is called a capital utilization test that measures how profit before interest and income tax was earned on the total capital employed by the business.

What are Independent Auditors?

Independent CPA auditors are like referees in the financial reporting arena. The CPA comes in, does an audit of the business's accounting system and methods and gives a report that is attached to the company's financial statements. Publicly owned businesses are required to have their annual financial reports audited by independent CPA firms and any privately owned businesses have audits done as well because they know that an audit report will add credibility to their financial reports.

An auditor judges whether the business's accounting methods are in accordance with generally accepted accounting principles (GAAP). Generally everything is in place and the financial report is a reliable document. But at times an auditor will wave a yellow or red flag. Some indicators of potential trouble include when the business's capability to continue normal operations is in doubt because of what are known as financial exigencies, which could mean a low cash balance, unpaid overdue liabilities, or major lawsuits that the business doesn't have the cash to cover.

An auditor must exercise professional skepticism, meaning the auditor should challenge the accounting methods and reporting practices of the client in order to make sure that its financial statement conform with accounting standards and are not misleading - in short, that the financial statement are fairly presented. Indeed, the words "fairly presented" are the exact words used in the auditor's report.

A good auditor need technical know-how, but also needs to know how to be tough on the accounting methods of the client. His job is to be the agent of the shareholders and other users of the business's financial report. It's incumbent on an auditor to strictly uphold GAAP, and not let any irregularities slide.

There are a number of well-known companies that engaged in accounting fraud recently and that fraud was not discovered by the CPA auditors. Enron is one of these companies. In this case, the auditing firm, Arthur Anderson was found guilty of obstruction of justice because it destroyed audit evidence.

What is Accounting Fraud?

Accounting fraud is a deliberate and improper manipulation of the recording of sales revenue and/or expenses in order to make a company's profit performance appear better than it actually is. Some things that companies do that can constitute fraud are:

--Not listing prepaid expenses or other incidental assets

--Not showing certain classifications of current assets and/or liabilities

--Collapsing short- and long-term debt into one amount.

Over-recording sales revenue is the most common technique of accounting fraud. A business may ship products to customers that they haven't ordered, knowing that those customers will return the products after the end of the year. Until the returns are made, the business records the shipments as if they were actual sales. Or a business may engage in channel stuffing. It delivers products to dealers or final customers that they really don't want, but business makes deals on the side that provide incentives and special privileges if the dealers or customers don't object to taking premature delivery of the products. A business may also delay recording products that have been returned by customers to avoid recognizing these offsets against sales revenue in the current year.

The other way a business commits accounting fraud is by under-recording expenses, such as not recording depreciation expense. Or a business may choose not to record all of its cost of goods sold expense fore the sales made during a period. This would make the gross margin higher, but the business's inventory asset would include products that actually are not in inventory because they've been delivered to customers.

A business might also choose not to record asset losses that should be recognized, such as uncollectible accounts receivable, or it might not write down inventory under the lower of cost or market rule. A business might also not record the full amount of the liability for an expense, making that liability understated in the company's balance sheet. Its profit, therefore, would be overstated.

What Does an Audit Do?

If a business breaks the rules of accounting and ethics, it can be liable for legal sanctions against it. It can deliberately deceive its investors and lenders with false or misleading numbers in its financial report. That's where audits come in. Audits are one means of keeping misleading financial reporting to a minimum. CPA auditors are like highway patrol officers who enforce traffic laws and issue tickets to keep speeding to a minimum. An audit exam can uncover problems that the business was not aware of.

After completing an audit examination, the CPA prepares a short report stating that the business has prepared its financial statements, according to generally accepted accounting principles (GAAP), or where it has not. All businesses that are publicly traded are required to have annual audits by independent CPAs. Those companies whose stocks are listed on the New York Stock Exchange or Nasdaq must be audited by outside CPA firms. For a publicly traded company, the expense of conducting an annual audit is the cost of doing business; it's the price a company pays for going into public markets for its capital and for having its shares traded in the public venue.

Although federal law doesn't require audits for private businesses, banks and other lenders to private businesses may insist on audited financial statements. If the lenders don't require audited statements, a business's owners have to decide whether an audit is a good investment. Instead of an audit, which they can't really afford, many smaller businesses have an outside CPA come in on a regular basis to look over their accounting methods and give advice on their financial reporting. But unless a CPA has done an audit, he or she has to be very careful not to express an opinion of the external financial statements. Without a careful examination of the evidence supporting the amounts reported in the financial statements, the CPA is in no position to give an opinion on the financial statements prepared from the accounts of the business.

What Does an Audit Report Contain?

Most audit reports on financial statements give the business a clean bill of health, or a clean opinion. At the other end of the spectrum, the auditor may state that the financial statements are misleading and should not be relied upon. This negative audit report is called an adverse opinion. That's the big stick that auditors carry. They have the power to give a company's financial statements an adverse opinion and no business wants that. The threat of an adverse opinion almost always motivates a business to give way to the auditor and change its accounting or disclosure in order to avoid getting the kiss of death of an adverse opinion. An adverse audit opinion says that the financial statements of the business are misleading. The SEC does not tolerate adverse opinions by auditors of public businesses; it would suspend trading in a company's stock share if the company received an adverse opinion from its CPA auditor.

One modification to an auditor's report is very serious - when the CPA firm says that it has substantial doubts about the capability of the business to continue as a going concern. A going concern is a business that has sufficient financial wherewithal and momentum to continue it normal operations into the foreseeable future and would be able to absorb a bad turn of events without having to default on its liabilities. A going concern does not face an imminent financial crisis or any pressing financial emergency. A business could be under some financial distress but overall still be judged a going concern. Unless there is evidence to the contrary, the CPA auditor assumes that the business is a going concern. If an auditor has serious concerns about whether the business is a going concern, these doubts are spelled out in the auditor's report.

How is Accounting Used in Business?

It might seem obvious, but in managing a business, it's important to understand how the business makes a profit. A company needs a good business model and a good profit model. A business sells products or services and earns a certain amount of margin on each unit sold. The number of units sold is the sales volume during the reporting period. The business subtracts the amount of fixed expenses for the period, which gives them the operating profit before interest and income tax.

It's important not to confuse profit with cash flow. Profit equals sales revenue minus expenses. A business manager shouldn't assume that sales revenue equals cash inflow and that expenses equal cash outflows. In recording sales revenue, cash or another asset is increased. The asset accounts receivable is increased in recording revenue for sales made on credit. Many expenses are recorded by decreasing an asset other than cash. For example, cost of goods sold is recorded with a decrease to the inventory asset and depreciation expense is recorded with a decrease to the book value of fixed assets. Also, some expenses are recorded with an increase in the accounts payable liability or an increase in the accrued expenses payable liability.

Remember that some budgeting is better than none. Budgeting provides important advantages, like understanding the profit dynamics and the financial structure of the business. It also helps for planning for changes in the upcoming reporting period. Budgeting forces a business manager to focus on the factors that need to be improved to increase profit. A well-designed management profit and loss report provides the essential framework for budgeting profit. It's always a good idea to look ahead to the coming year. If nothing else, at least plug the numbers in your profit report for sales volume, sales prices, product costs and other expense and see how your projected profit looks for the coming year.

How to Set Up a Simplified Accounting System for Your Business

A lot of home businesses fail because they lack the necessary financial system to track down the flow of their money. More often than not, home based business owners are not really very keen at keeping their books of accounts, thinking that as long as money keeps coming in, they will be alright.
Unfortunately, things are not really that simple when you are engaged in business. If you want to stay in business for a long time, you will need to keep track of your financial flow for your own use and for taxation purposes. Note that if you do not keep track of your income, sooner or later the IRS will be unto you and you will get into big trouble.

Setting up your own simplified bookkeeping system is not really very complicated. If you like to keep your records in your computer, you might want to buy accounting software or just simply use whatever programs that will allow you to make a spreadsheet in your computer to record your daily transactions.

However, you have some money to spare for an accounting program, it would be better to have one. There is a number of easy to use accounting software being sold in the market today. The good thing about these accounting programs is that you do not need to worry about balancing your books of accounts. You simply input all your data in one page and the program will run on its own. Most accounting programs will automatically perform the different accounting process and will immediately update your statements of accounts. Retrieving data from an accounting program is also easy.

All you need to do is to go to it archives and select which ones you want to see. For instance, if you want to know how much your net income is for the month, you simply pull-out the income statement page and you will see your income instantly. Another advantage of using a computer accounting program is that you get rid of all the papers and ledgers in your workplace.

Now, in case you are not comfortable using your computer to balance your books, then you just have to you things the old-fashioned way. What if you do not know anything about accounting processes? Never mind if you are not good in accounting and balancing statements of accounts, just keep a simplified records of your transactions. A three column worksheet will do nicely. You can easily find this type of worksheet in the bookstore. When dividing your worksheet, you can have one column for all the money you received in connection with the business, another column for all the money that you spend for your business and the third column will be for your running balance.

Small Business Tax Issues for the Self-Employed

The United States is a nation of entrepreneurs. There are literally tens of millions of self-employed individuals that enjoy pursuing their dream business. Of course, few of us enjoy the paperwork and confusing tax issues that arise from owning your own business.

Many self-employed individuals are considered "sole proprietors" or "independent contractors" for legal and tax purposes. This is true regardless of whether you are turning a hobby into a business, selling an indispensable widget or providing services to others. As a self-employed person, you report business revenue results on your personal income tax return. Following are a few guidelines and issues you should keep in mind if you are pursuing your entrepreneurial spirit.

Schedule C – Form 1040.
As a self-employed person, you are required to report your business profits or losses on Schedule C of Form 1040. The income earned through your business is taxable to you as an individual. This is true even if you do not withdraw any money from the business. While you are required to report your gross revenues, you are also allowed to deduct business expenses incurred in generating that revenue. If your business efforts result in a loss, the loss will generally be deductible against your total income from all sources, subject to special rules relating to whether your business is considered a hobby and whether you have anything "at risk."

Home-Based Business
Many self-employed individuals work out of their home and are entitled to deduct a percentage of certain home costs that are applicable to the portion of the home that is used as your office. This can include payments for utilities, telephone services, etc. You may also be eligible to claim these deductions if you perform administrative tasks from your home or store inventory there. If you work out of your home and have an additional office at another location, you also may be able to convert your commuting expenses between the two locations into deductible transportation expenses. Since most self-employed individuals find themselves working more than the traditional 40-hour week, there are a significant number of advantageous deductions that can be claimed. Unfortunately, we find that most self-employed individuals miss these deductions because they are unaware of them.

Self-Employment Taxes – The Bad News

A negative aspect to being self-employed is the self-employment tax. All salaried individuals are subject to automatic deductions from their paycheck including FICA, etc. In that many self-employed individuals often do not run a formal payroll for themselves, the government must recapture these taxes through the self-employment tax. Simply put, you are required to pay self-employment taxes at a rate of 15.3% on your net earnings up to $87,900 for 2004. For net income in excess of $87,900, you will pay further taxes at a rate of 2.9% on the excess.

In an interesting twist that reveals the confusing nature of the tax code, you are allowed a partial deduction for the self-employment tax. Simply put, you are allowed to deduct one-half of your self-employment taxes from your gross income. For example, if you pay $10,000 in self-employment taxes, you are allowed a deduction on your 1040 return of $5,000. Many self-employed individuals miss this deduction and pay more money to taxes than needed.

Health Insurance Deduction

This used to be a very messy area for self-employed individuals, to wit, you received little tax relief when it came to your health insurance bill. This was a particular burden for small business owners when considering the astronomical cost of health insurance. All of this has changed and may continue to change with regard to new health insurance laws, rules, mandates, and extensions. You can attempt to stay on top of this information or ask your licensed health insurance professional in order to take the most advantage of these laws.

If you're self-employed or a small company, we suggest asking your licensed health insurance broker for the right plan for you. A high deductible, but low premium plan combined with an HSA (health savings account) can be optimal. It can act as a tax haven for you rather than a tax burden for others. It is essentially an IRA for your health expenses up to your deductible amount until regular insurance kicks in in case of emergencies. You'll likely be allowed several thousand dollars per year in your account and, as of now, it can accrue year after year. You will likely have a high deductible, but low premiums. Even in the event that you do have to use up all of the deductible, in combination with the lower premiums, it may be possible that you can still come out ahead rather than having a higher premium plan throughout the year.

You can take this type of plan and combine it with a fee for service doctor in your area. You can pay for your routine medical expenses out of this account with tax free dollars. Save the insurance for the real emergencies.

No Withholding Tax
Unlike a salaried employee, you are not subject to withholding tax on your paycheck. While this sounds great, you are required to make quarterly estimated tax payments. If you fail to make the payments, you are subject to a penalty, but the penalty is not the biggest concern.

A potential and dangerous pitfall of being self-employed is failing to pay quarterly estimated taxes and then getting caught at the end of the year without sufficient funds to pay your taxes. The IRS is not going to be happy if you fail to pay your taxes and you will suffer the consequences in the form of penalties and interest. Making sure you pay quarterly estimated taxes helps avoid this situation and it is highly recommended that you follow this course of action.

Record Keeping
You must maintain complete records of all business income and expenses. Simply put, document everything. Create a filing system for each month and file every receipt, etc. All business travel expenses must be documented, including auto mileage you incur when performing business tasks. Office supply stores sell business mileage books that you can keep in your car and use whenever you travel. If you have any doubt about documenting something, just do it!

As a self-employed individual, your focus and time is spent on making your business successful. Your focus is not on the complexities of the tax code and how to limit the amount of taxes you owe. If any of the information in this article is new to you, then it is highly likely you have paid far more in taxes than required.

Taxes

Consult with your accountant and set up all necessary federal and state tax accounts. Some accountants/bookkeepers will come in one day per week and take care of your transactions for the week all in one shot. Better yet, they can monitor your transactions and work with you virtually. As a matter of fact, I've never even met our bookkeeper in person Sometimes you can find a personal assistant or concierge that can do bookkeeping for you. If you have employees, there will be further accounts to set up. Paying your estimated taxes on a quarterly basis will most likely be easiest and economical. You can find these professionals in your local organizations like networking groups and chamber of commerce.

Top 7 Small Business Tax Tips

Here are seven ways for owners of small businesses to save money on their taxes.

1. Incorporate Yourself: If you`re still a proprietor or partner of a business, it`s time to incorporate yourself. Not only will you limit your liability, but you may enjoy lower tax rates on small business income and other tax advantages as well.

2. Be Home Based: If possible, continue (or switch to) being a home based business. Not only will you keep your overhead down, but you will be able to write-off (or deduct) the business use of your home.

3. Income Split: Pay reasonable wages to your spouse and children. In this way, you can legally divert income taxed at your higher rate to your family members that are in a lower tax bracket.

4. Rearrange Your Affairs For Maximum Tax Savings: Can you make some changes to turn your hobby into a moneymaking business? Can you use that extra room in your house as a home office for your business? Can you arrange to use your car more for business purposes? Can you arrange for more of your entertainment expenses to be

business   related?

5. Document Your Expenses Well: Do you document your expenses well so that they would survive a tax audit? Have you kept a mileage log so that you can prove the percentage business use you claim for your vehicle? Have you kept receipts for all your entertainment expenses and listed the business purpose on the back of each receipt?

6. Be Punctual: File all returns and pay all taxes due (income, payroll, sales, et cetera) on time. This way, you avoid expensive late filing (and payment) penalties and interest.

7. Develop a Tax Planning Mindset: Some people only worry about their taxes during tax season. However, you will save a fortune in taxes, legally, if you make tax planning your year-round concern. Do you make business and personal purchases, investments, and other expenditures with tax savings in mind? You should start to think about and track these kinds of expenses to come out ahead in the long run.

Download Expense Estimate Worksheet
http://goo.gl/uwIQJz

Download Profitability Analysis Worksheet
http://goo.gl/Dq9IhL

Simple 3 Column Printable Ledger Paper
http://goo.gl/sHulD9

Use the worksheet below to track your monthly sales pace.
Date: March 2008   * To find pace, divide your month total with the
Goal: $60,000.00   Example: to find the pace on day 9 first divide

	New Sales	Pace	Set	Show	Close
Day 1	$ 400.00	$ 12,400.00	2	1	1
Day 2	$ 1,200.00	$ 24,800.00	5	3	2
Day 3	$ 650.00	$ 23,250.00	3	2	2
Day 4	$ 900.00	$ 24,412.50	1	1	1
Day 5	$ 4,600.00	$ 48,050.00	5	3	3
Day 6	$ 7,300.00	$ 77,758.33	6	4	3
Day 7	$ -	$ 66,650.00	2	1	0
Day 8	$ 400.00	$ 59,868.75	1	1	1
Day 9	$ 1,000.00		2	2	2
Day 10	$ -				
Day 11	$ -				
Day 12	$ -				
Day 13	$ -				
Day 14	$ -				
Day 15	$ -				
Day 16	$ -				
Day 17	$ -				
Day 18	$ -				
Day 19	$ -				
Day 20	$ -				
Day 21	$ -				
Day 22	$ -				
Day 23	$ -				
Day 24	$ -				
Day 25	$ -				
Day 26	$ -				
Day 27	$ -				
Day 28	$ -				
Day 29	$ -				
Day 30	$ -				
Day 31	$ -				
TOTAL	$ 16,450.00		27	18	15
	Total Sales		Set	Show	Close

Bank Account

Go to your favorite local bank (they aren't that much different) and set up a business checking account and merchant services to accept credit cards and, most importantly, EFT (electronic funds transfer) or ARB (automatic recurring billing). Preferably go to one where you have a contact working there. Sometimes a local credit union can be a good option too and maybe better in some instances than the larger banks. See if you can set up a business line of credit at that visit as well for a little extra cushion in the future. Based on our experience, credit unions may not be as good as dealing with small business as some other commercial banks are, but it's worth looking into first. Setting up this account is where you will need the EIN number you get from the IRS.

Up until this point, you may not have much money to open the account with. That's ok too. We used the revenue from our first client to open our account. She paid us with a check and we deposited it soon thereafter.

If you're really bootstrapping, you may be able to make use of some online resources early on like Paypal or maybe even Google Checkout. Paypal has a virtual terminal option and a subscription feature for recurring billing of your clients. More on that later. Additionally, they have merchant services like the web code for buttons you can simply cut and paste into your website as you develop it.

Insurance

You'll need the right insurance and maybe bonding for your industry and business insurance. Check with a local independent insurance agent or your bank can possibly offer one of these programs.

Personal Finance

Getting money out of your business is sometimes tricky. We suggest setting up an automatic billing model in which your clients are charged twice a month either on the first or the 15th of the month. You can tie your own pay in with these payments so that you can more closely replicate a regular pay check. That's one of the hardest things for entrepreneurs to do. The more regular and predictable your revenue, the easier it will be to pay yourself regularly. This is critical if you are to have your business serve your daily, weekly, monthly needs. If you have a simple set up like an LLC, you will take a draw or distribution from the business bank account as your pay. Be sure to put a little away for estimated quarterly taxes or for the end of the tax year. You will be taxed personally in what is called a pass through fashion. Meaning your business is the entity being passed through with regard to imposed taxes onto you personally. Once you have your clients on automatic billing, put yourself on automatic payments too.

Personal Budget. First, in order to make sure that you're profiting at home, you'll need a personal budget so your expenses don't exceed your income which can vary with your own business. This is the equivalent of counting calories for your clients. Budgets are terrible and boring, but they have to be done. Thankfully, more and more technology is making it easier for us. The link at the beginning of this paragraph is to any number of templates you might want to choose from in Google Drive. Choose one that you find simple to use and appropriate for you. Record your monthly transactions as accurately as you can to get an idea of where your money is going. You can also use services like www.mint.com which will draw transactions in directly from your online accounts you connect.

Checking account. This is where you will conduct most of your personal transactions from. We suggest looking for a local credit union. Although credit unions don't seem to be good with business bank accounts, they are good with personal accounts. This may be a better option than bigger banks as you'll get all the benefits and maybe some better rates and better service. Your share (savings) account will give you a share in the union. The board will also likely be elected. So you'll have more power and more say in your local financial institution in which you choose to do business. You should have a check/debit card that works like a credit card and maybe a check book although more and more people are doing everything digitally these days.

Savings account or rainy day fund. You can keep this account in the same place you'll have your checking account. This is an account you can keep for larger expenses in which you save up for or for unforeseen circumstances or emergencies. This may be a good place to keep your funds you'll need should something happen to your business or you become incapacitated in some way. Financial experts recommend differing total amounts you want to keep in it that range anywhere from three to 12 months. Considering most Americans save very little, even a three month emergency fund can provide a very small safety net for you other people don't have. This is a liquid account you should be able to access quickly and easily and transfer money into and out of almost immediately. You can fund this account regularly and automatically with a portion of your pay too.

Credit account. Once again, you can most likely get a line of credit from the same institution you choose to have checking and savings accounts. A no annual fee, low interest credit card can be good to keep on hand, but only for use in emergencies. Or, use it to build credit or earn rewards or points or miles, but be certain that you can pay it off in full each month or carry a very small balance.

Investment account/money market. A simple and easy way to set this up is through a company [David Bach recommends in his book, The Automatic Millionaire.](#) Sharebuilder. www.sharebuilder.com. You can set up an individual investment account for paper investments. This account also contains with it, a money market account in which you can save money or fund your investments from. A money market account, although not insured, is like a savings account. It still carries risk and the possibility exists that it could lose money, but along with that small risk is the possibility of a slightly higher return than your typical savings account. This is still a liquid account and funds you can get to relatively quickly, but may require 3-5 business days to process transfers to or from other accounts. For investments, you'll want a diversified portfolio across different market sectors. The brokerage you choose may have suggested portfolios based on things like your risk tolerance and age. You can also ask your financial advisor for a specific portfolio. It can be made up of stocks, bonds, mutual funds, exchange traded funds (ETF's), among others.

Retirement account. IRA or 401(k). You will need a retirement account. If you're working for yourself, you will not have an employer to pay you a pension or set up your 401(k) for you. You can speak with one of their customer service reps at Sharebuilder and you may be able to set up a 401(k) for yourself and for any employees you may currently have or have in the future.

You may also choose to set up an Individual Retirement Account or IRA. There are generally two kinds, a traditional and a Roth. You will probably want a Roth IRA. The difference is when the money is taxed. With a traditional IRA account, it is tax deferred. The money is put in non-taxed and then taxed when you withdraw it when you are 65 or older. A Roth IRA is taxed dollars that you can withdraw later without being taxed again after it has compounded. Essentially, it is do you want to be taxed now or later? I personally prefer the Roth IRA because who knows what the tax code will be like decades from now. They could always change it, but I prefer to put it in now under the laws we currently have.

Precious metals. This is a little bit of a wild card. Precious metals can make up around to five or 10% of your invested dollars. It adds another layer of diversification and protection from inflation. Inflation is like a tax in that it makes the value of all the dollars we currently have go down because there is now more paper currency in circulation without being backed up by anything. And that anything is supposed to be gold and silver, but we got off of that system some time ago. Now, you can invest in gold and silver and other metals to act as a hedge against inflationary time period or, god forbid, a major economic disaster. At present time of writing this, a simple silver one dollar coin is actually worth about $21 dollars simply because of the value of the metal it is made from. An equal amount of gold is over $1300 Generally speaking, when the stock market does well, precious metals go down. When the stock market is doing poorly, or inflation is high, gold and silver do very well. Precious metals also tend to do well when there is uncertainty in other areas of the economy or geopolitical turmoil in the world like in oil producing nations. Again, precious metals act mostly like a hedge or protection against these things.

The formula for determining profit on which budgets are based is **Income – Expenses = Profit.**

It isn't complicated and you don't need to be a rocket scientist to figure out that there are two ways to improve your profit.

1. increase income or
2. decrease expenses.

If you can figure out how to do both simultaneously, please let us know.
It would be nice to just crank up the burners and make more money, wouldn't it? Unfortunately increasing income is much harder than decreasing expenses when it comes to improving your bottom line.

At least once in a lifetime need is great and resources are few. This is particularly so if you make frequent transitions from one income stream to others. It can be hard enough to make ends meet on a decent wage with a single job. When times get tough and the money is not there to meet the need, a person can easily despair.

There is no magic formula for coming up with on-the-spot cash. But you can sleep better at night with good financial control and a plan of action should emergency funds be needed.

How to Cope with a Cash Crisis

Here's how to assess your situation and get back on your feet.

Without warning your roof begins to leak. Your hot water heater shuts down, your computer blows up, the clutch needs to be replaced and your son books his wedding on the Island of Oahu – in the same week! Oh, and your boss advises that a round of layoffs, that includes your job, is coming. Stunned and pondering an exit strategy a friendly letter arrives from the IRS explaining that you miscalculated your taxes in 1996, and your house is no longer your own. What do you do?

The above scenario looks like a financial emergency of biblical proportions. You can restore your financial life and equilibrium—and perhaps even fend off future misfortune—without having to sell your soul.

Money woes are usually accompanied by crippling emotional setbacks. This is particularly true of men who characteristically tie their self-worth to earning power. You will need to cope very well if you hope to make a solid financial comeback.

Whenever a money emergency hits, the ability of the individual to deal with huge amounts of stress that will keep things steady. Calm and rational study of each problem as it arises may lessen the feeling of being overwhelmed.

Calm must take center stage. You must *never* allow yourself the luxury of panic. No one is there to take over. It's just you. The more you panic, the less effective you will be. You need to keep a clear head to formulate an appropriate plan. Be aware of your own tendency to sabotage plans through panic. The first step in managing a money emergency is to remaining calm and optimistic. Don't act right away or you will inevitably make a mistake! Before you manage your finances again, you have to manage your emotions. Before you can begin your comeback plan you must regain your balance.

If your emergency demands quick action, think first about seeking advice from a debt counselor, money coach or financial planner. Whenever possible seek help from a financially-perceptive friend or family member.

Time to Crunch Some Numbers

The first step is to step back! Assess the damage. A big mistake often made in the throes of a financial crisis is failure to look clearly at the situation.

It is easy to be overwhelmed. However, totaling up the damage serves two important purposes. First, you need to know exactly how much you owe, how much money you have in hand and what it will take to cover the distance between the two. Second, you want to avoid other mishaps, such as penalties, further repairs, or missed deadlines.
If you are not properly prepared, you must prepare on the spot. Any type of money crisis creates a feeling of being cornered. It would be better to be prepared, but how likely is that?

Most people will be somewhat prepared. If the crisis is not too dire, they will be able to handle it. Others may be sunk from the get go. Ideally, you would not be overwhelmed because you have a good plan of action, no matter how small. Unexpected expenses could be covered by funds in the irregular expenses of any good budget. Unfortunately, your emergency stash may not be enough. You would not be alone in this.

About this time you might turn to plastic for relief. Resist this urge. It will merely transfer the problem from one pocket to another.

However, if you are sure you can handle credit card debt to deal with a cash emergency, you need to ensure you can pay them off. Otherwise, why add yet another debt?

Think well before borrowing from your 401(k) or Income Retirement Account. There are loopholes that allow this, but also hidden costs, quite apart from potential taxes, penalties and other consequences. Keep in mind that if you were to lose your job, you'd have to repay the loan immediately, or be taxed as though it was a withdrawal. This remedy could be costly in the long run.

14 GROWTH AND CONVEYING YOUR VISION TO OTHERS

Hiring employees

There is an upper limit to what we can do ourselves. In which case, when it comes time, you may want to try to scale your business up further by replicating yourself or hiring more employees to work with you. This can also free you up to hopefully move out of your daily training responsibilities and focus more on growing more of the revenue generating parts of your business. This is known as working ON your business rather than working IN your business. It's a real challenge for all entrepreneurs, but you'll want to start to think that way if you ever want your business to grow to something beyond just you or if you'd like to sell it one day.

It is critically important that you get the right people working for you early on. Hire slow and fire fast. You want them to be on board with your mission and vision of your company. Without that critical piece, they aren't going to feel a part of something bigger and they will be more concerned with what is going to directly benefit them individually rather than the team or organization as a whole. Your company will have not only a mission and vision, but a set of *core values*. Take the time to clearly establish these and use this in your hiring process. What is most important to you in creating the company culture you'd like when brining in additional people? Once a culture is corrupted or becomes toxic, it is very hard to reverse. It may help if you already have some form of good relationship with the potential new hires you bring in to interview.

We suggest taking a multi-step approach to new hires. Do not hire right after the first meeting. You may even want to implement an initial training process like an internship or apprenticeship for all new prospective hires. This will give you time to really weed out who is not serious or aligned with your mission, vision, and values.

If your whole staff has the same values and can see your long term vision, you'll have a great start to forming a cohesive team and positive company culture.

Three Step Hiring Process

1. Have the prospective employee fill out an application and submit a resume and cover letter. Right away, you can weed out many poor candidates by asking them to snail mail or fax a copy of their resume in addition to submitting through electronic formats. What this does is tell you a little more of who is serious and who isn't. Who can follow specific directions. If they are willing to take the extra 2 minutes to send a fax or put a stamp on an envelope, they may be a more serious candidate than those just blasting generic resumes to anyone and everyone.

2. Set up a phone interview. Preferably with a manager. Be sure that they are familiar with your company, that they know who you are, what you do, and what you are all about. Be sure they have visited your company website. You can spend most of this time talking at the prospect. Mostly conveying what your core values are and what your company culture is like. If they don't think this is right for them or they don't agree with some of the values, they may not be a good fit and there's no need to go any further.

3. If the prospective employee has made it this far, it is a good opportunity to have them come in for an in person interview. You can meet with them as the boss or owner. Be sure to recap and review what you'd already talked about. But, this meeting is so that you can learn more about them. Most of this time is for them to inform you about themselves. Listen and learn to see if you still believe they are a good candidate.

If all seems well after this meeting, send them home and follow up with them in the next two days after you've had an opportunity to think about it and sleep on it. If you still believe this person will be a good fit and they are still eager to come aboard, you can begin their intake process. They can be started on your in house training program if you have one (you should). This can be paid or unpaid initial training, your choice. And be sure to establish that all new hires are on a 90 day probationary period in case they don't work out in the short term.

Below, we will give you some of the tools you'll need to get started bringing on potential new hires.

Click here to download an **Employee Application Form**
http://goo.gl/3TBvBn

Job Description

Company Name

Job Title:	Job Code:
Department:	Job Grade:
Revision Date:	Fair Labor Standards Act (FLSA):

Position Overview

Essential Job Functions

Non-essential Job Functions

Requirements

Other Skills/Abilities

NOTE: This job description is not intended to be all-inclusive. Employee may perform other related duties as negotiated to meet the ongoing needs of the organization.

Employee Evaluation

1. What goals did you accomplish since your last evaluation (or hire)?
2. What goals were you unable to accomplish and what hindered you from achieving them?
3. What goals will you set for the next period?
4. What resources do you need from the organization to achieve these goals?
5. Based on YOUR personal satisfaction with your job (workload, environment, pay, challenge, etc.) how would you rate your satisfaction from 1 (poor) to 10 (excellent.)

1 2 3 4 5 6 7 8 9 10

*You do have to stress that question #5 is not how well they think they're doing their job, but how satisfied they are with the job.

This is a simple, but very effective review process you can do with staff members 90 days after hire and every 6 months thereafter. It's the simplicity that is the beauty. It won't take all day to do and you'll likely get truthful and accurate feedback from the employee.

Exit Interview

Name: Date:

	Strongly Agree	Agree	Neutral	Disagree	Strongly Disagree	N/A
Overall this job met my expectations and provided me with information I can use.	☐	☐	☐	☐	☐	☐
The projects were interesting and relevant to my career	☐	☐	☐	☐	☐	☐

objectives.						
The representative devoted enough time to me, my questions, and the experience in general.	☐	☐	☐	☐	☐	☐
Overall I would recommend this job to another person.	☐	☐	☐	☐	☐	☐

Which aspect did you enjoy the most? Why?

___

Which aspect did you enjoy the least? Why?

___

Was the workload too much, too little, or just about right?

___

Based on your experience with us, what do you think it takes to succeed at this company?

___

How do you generally feel about this company?

___

What can we do to improve this experience for future employees?

Is there anything else about your experience here that you'd like to share?

May we contact you in the future for follow-up, regarding leads, or for job opportunities within or outside our company?

☐ Yes
☐ No

15 EXIT, LIFECYCLE, END GAME

At some point, you're not going to be running your business yourself. It will have a lifecycle for you. You may have birthed it, but the entity may not die with you. It could, that's certainly a possibility. Other options would be that you could eventually have it well managed and you remain an absentee owner. You'd still have ownership and responsibility over it. It could still feed your lifestyle and provide you income.

You may choose to sell off a majority ownership of it and remain a silent partner while someone else runs it. You may take the company public and sell millions of shares of it on the stock market. You may sell it off completely for a windfall profit. You may sell it and agree to stay on as an employee or consultant for an additional two years. Or you may simply and quietly close it down when the time is right. Or you may go out of business financially.

In any case, you'll need to decide what to do when the time is right or when the option presents itself. It is much easier to have this in your overall vision and plan from the beginning and you can adjust as you go and acquire new information.

Ideally, the end result will again be in line with how you want your business to feed your life. Maybe it's a career and you don't want to work in retirement. Maybe it's a retirement source of activity. Maybe it's a retirement vehicle. It's up to you.

Decide what you want ahead of time, to the best of your ability, given the information you have at the time and include this in your business plan under exit strategy.

The IRS has a helpful checklist for closing a business:

"**Closing a Business Checklist**

There are typical actions that are taken when closing a business. You must file an annual return for the year you go out of business. If you have employees, you must file the final employment tax returns, in addition to making final federal tax deposits of these taxes. Also attach a statement to your return showing the name of the person keeping the payroll records and the address where those records will be kept.

The annual tax return for a partnership, corporation, S corporation, limited liability company or trust includes check boxes near the top front page just below the entity information. For the tax year in which your business ceases to exist, check the box that indicates this tax return is a final return. If there are Schedule K-1s, repeat the same procedure on the Schedule K-1.

You will also need to file returns to report disposing of business property, reporting the exchange of like-kind property, and/or changing the form of your business. If you do not have a pre-printed envelope in which to send your taxes, refer to the Where To File page for a list of addresses. Below is a list of typical actions to take when closing a business, depending on your type of business structure:

Checklist
- **Make final federal tax deposits**
    - Electronic Federal Tax Paying System (EFTPS)
- **File final quarterly or annual employment tax form.**
    - Form 940, Employer's Annual Federal Unemployment (FUTA) Tax Return (PDF)
    - Form 941, Employer's Quarterly Federal Tax Return (PDF)
    - Form 943, Employer's Annual Tax Return for Agricultural Employees (PDF)
    - Form 943-A, Agricultural Employer's Record of Federal Tax Liability (PDF)
- **Issue final wage and withholding information to employees**
    - Form W-2, Wage and Tax Statement (PDF)

- **Report information from W-2s issued.**
    - Form W-3, Transmittal of Income and Tax Statements (PDF)
- **File final tip income and allocated tips information return.**
    - Form 8027, Employer's Annual Information Return of Tip Income and Allocated Tips (PDF)
- **Report capital gains or losses.**
    - Form 1040, U.S. Individual Income Tax Return (PDF)
    - Form 1065, U.S. Partnership Return of Income (PDF)
    - Form 1120 (Schedule D), Capital Gains and Losses (PDF)
- **Report partner's/shareholder's shares.**
    - Form 1065 (Schedule K-1), Partner's Share of Income, Credits, Deductions, etc. (PDF)
    - Form 1120S (Schedule K-1), Shareholder's Share of Income, Credits, Deductions, etc. (PDF)
- **File final employee pension/benefit plan.**
    - Form 5500, Annual Return/Report of Employee Benefit Plan
- **Issue payment information to sub-contractors.**
    - Form 1099-MISC, Miscellaneous Income (PDF)
- **Report information from 1099s issued.**
    - Form 1096, Annual Summary and Transmittal of U.S. Information Returns (PDF)
- **Report corporate dissolution or liquidation.**
    - Form 966, Corporate Dissolution or Liquidation (PDF)
- **Consider allowing S corporation election to terminate.**
    - Form 1120S, Instructions (PDF)
- **Report business asset sales.**
    - Form 8594, Asset Acquisition Statement (PDF)
- **Report the sale or exchange of property used in your trade or business.**
    - Form 4797, Sales of Business Property (PDF)"

Reference: http://www.irs.gov/Businesses/Small-Businesses-&-Self-Employed/Closing-a-Business-Checklist

16 PUTTING IT ALTOGETHER

Organization

To help you keep things straight, click here to download a zip file with categorized folders in which to store your business documents and tools.   http://goo.gl/hQdGQ8 Back these systems up in a safe place, preferably online, so you won't lose your business processes should something happen to your computer. Be extra careful with any sensitive data like client credit card numbers and make sure they are in a secure place.

Business Performance Tracker Checklist

For each question, answer Yes or No

Statement/Question	Answer	Solutions/Resources
You have the interest and drive to start a business in this field.		
You have a good mix of technical skills and business sense.		

You have researched your local market and determined that you have a viable idea or opportunity differentiated from the competition.		
You have a plan in place covering the short term and long term vision.		
You have a clear model and clearly defined audience or niche in which to serve.		
You have incorporated your business or are operating as a sole proprietor.		
You have the appropriate classification of who is an employee or contractor.		
You have an accurate and reliable bookkeeping and accounting system in place.		
You can know the state of your business finances at any time.		
Your business has a cash cushion.		
You have budgets set up.		
You keep track of your business expenses.		
You understand how you and your business is taxed. You have access to legal services.		
You are properly insured and/or bonded.		

Your personal finances are in line for when you take money out of your business.		
Everyone in your organization has a clear role and responsibilities in writing.		
You have a clearly established sales system.		
You diversify with other revenue streams.		
You have a marketing plan with an established schedule and systems.		
You have good retention of clients and receive a good amount of regular referrals.		
You have clear and visible written policies in place that you and clients abide by.		
You have a set operating methodology in place that is reproducible by anyone.		
You have a set hiring process, in line with your core values to find the right people.		
You have a set staff training procedure and regular meetings in place.		

If you answered no to any of the above questions, place a task in your to do list that works toward resolving this issue until you have a reliable system in place.

Automation

It's a good idea to automate as many processes in your business as you possibly can. If you're working solo, you'll definitely be responsible for every aspect of your business. Sometimes, there may not be enough hours in the day or week for you to do them all.

Worse would be where you're stuck doing mundane tasks that still have to be done, but it gets to where it is competing for time you could be making sales and producing revenue for your company. There are many ways you can automate or outsource functions of your business so that you can focus on what really needs to be done or what you do best and enjoy. Good things to automate or outsource in your business include:

- Administrative tasks
- Bookkeeping
- Accounting
- Market research
- Customer service
- E-commerce
- Customer relationship management
- Sales
- Marketing
- Shipping
- Copy writing
- PR
- Business development

Essentially, you could automate or outsource almost anything in your business. Technology and good relationships or other firms can allow you to do that.

Potential Business Models

Freelancing and Consulting

When you think of a freelancer, what is the first thing that comes to mind? You probably think of a writer, novelist or journalist. You may have heard of freelance photographers. What about freelance software designers, freelance medical billing specialists, or even freelance scientific researchers?

These are jobs that have experienced massive growth in recent years as more and more people realize they can make far more money working as freelancers than they can working solely for their previous employer.

It sounds pretty good, doesn't it? You work in a field of expertise for quite a few years, gain practical experience then gradually make the switch from the full working day to becoming your own boss as a freelancer or consultant.

Is it really as easy as it sounds? Keep in mind there are quite a few freelancers who only work part time. This is not because they make a ton of money and need only work a couple of days per week. It's because they had trouble finding work in the past and needed a better career option. So here, freelancing or consulting is merely one stream for them.

However, this scenario need not apply to you if you are willing to do whatever it takes to become a freelancer. Eventually, you can become highly successful at what you do in this stream.

The first step in making that jump from an office to freelancing is deciding whether or not you have what it takes.

We all want to be our own boss, but do all of us possess the drive and dedication it can take to be successful without the watchful eye of a supervisor? Sadly, we don't. Therefore, you have to think about what makes you special in a world of freelancers or consultants.

Do you have a large enough skill set to enable you to stand out among the hordes of different people seeking the same work?

Do you have the time management skills necessary to run your own consulting operation and meet all deadlines set by your clients in the absence of your familiar structured work environment?

To start raking in the cash later you need to be willing to start off slowly along your new freelance path.

Don't quit your job just yet! Instead, begin your hunt for freelance work in your area of expertise on the internet with some informal market research.

Some skills, including the ability to write coherently or undertake software design for any type of client, are highly marketable.

Conversely, if you are only able to do tasks that are easily marketable, you may have a harder time finding work for a freelance operation.

Some of the most popular fields for consulting include writing, editing, photography, web and graphic design, software design, and architecture or drafting.

Once you have chosen your freelance field you need your first clients. Do not, however, start with any clients connected to your current job. Various laws prohibit what can effectively amount to stealing clients.

Instead, turn to your favorite search engine and hunt through forums and databases specifically designed for freelancers seeking work in a particular field. Ask your friends and family.

There are tons of different sites available that within about an hour may have yielded at least 10 bookmarks for potential employment as a freelancer.

With any free time, you can search each of your bookmarked websites to find the best-sounding freelance positions.

Initially, you may need to take a few low-paying jobs. They are useful in helping build your skill set as well as your portfolio and testimonials of your work.

They will also help you learn how to better manage your time, speed up your workflow, and help with internet-based research for projects.

The low-paying jobs will no doubt continue until you have assembled a massive list of satisfied clients. They will help you compete with other freelancers in your field in tandem with your low your rates and fees.

Eventually you will graduate into higher paying jobs and with it the realization that consulting or freelancing has significantly increased your income.

Pros and Cons

Working for yourself on a per client basis has both benefits and drawbacks that you need to research before you start.

Many people will tell you that leaving an office environment was the best thing they ever did. Others could not wait for each freelance project to end because they hated the stress of their assignments.

Here are some of the most common benefits and drawbacks you will face.

Benefits

The moment you decide to become a freelancer, you may be told how "cool" it is to be your own boss. You are in control of your work and nobody else (except your clients) can tell you what to do. If you don't want to work on Fridays you don't have to. Take any days off you want, but you must finish your projects by the deadline.

As your own boss, you have freedom to steer your life where you want it to go. You can plan your own schedules, choose the projects that you find enjoyable, charge any rate you please, and be almost totally self-sufficient.

Another big benefit of freelancing and consulting is that you can set your own dress code. If you find all your freelance work online, who is to say that you can't hang around in your pajamas or underwear all day? There is no sense in getting dressed up when you can just get out of bed, enjoy a cup of hot coffee and plop yourself down at the computer to start work. Consulting creates the opportunity to work in your own style and in total comfort.

A freelancer can potentially spend a lot more time with family and friends because there is no need to work on a strict office schedule. Spend time with your children when they get home from school, Ferry them to play dates or activities, meet your friends or have a date with your spouse whenever they are free.

The flexibility of a freelance income stream is second to none. There is practically no other job in the world that gives you both the spare time and the financial freedom to do what you want, when you want.

Finally, consulting has a near limitless income potential. Working for yourself means you can keep all of what you earn. Not a penny goes to anyone else (apart from taxes and expenses).

All profit belong to you but remember will likely need to re-invest a portion of it into your business to continue the hunt for clients. Furthermore, because you work on a per project basis, you can accept as many projects as you want to earn as much money as you see fit.

You are not salaried, so the more work you do, the more you get paid. This alone puts you directly in touch with the rewards from your work, unlike a specialized, salaried job. This can wake you from the zombie-like state of the "working dead."

Drawbacks

There are a few. Predominantly, you are not as financially stable as a salaried employee.

You need to manage your money yourself and ensure a stream of projects to make enough money to stay afloat financially. You must constantly market yourself for future work. And in some countries, such as the United States, you have to provide for your own healthcare.

These three factors create a feeling of fiscal insecurity for many people, and a deterrent because of the major financial risk involved.

There is also heavy competition in the world of freelancing. The internet has been both a blessing and a curse. On the one hand it has opened doors and made the world of consulting more accessible to anyone who has contemplated setting up on their own. On the other, the internet has increased competition for clients among freelancers and forced start-ups to offer very low rates for initial jobs.

How to Get into the Freelancing or Consulting Business

We have all read an article, seen a photograph, tinkered with some software, or visited a website that was designed by some type of freelancer.

Chances are that at some point we have all contemplated leaving our specialized jobs in large offices and starting afresh – alone. But, why don't we?

What holds so many of us back? Why do we allow ourselves to be tied to our employer as if some invisible shackles enslave us? What types of skills do we need to break free from typical nine to five shifts? All these questions need to be asked first.

Every year, far too many people quit their jobs to pursue a freelance career only to fail and have to crawl back to their previous employer for their job.

This unfortunate circumstance happens for one reason: the prospective freelancer had no idea what to expect. He was told he could be free, have as many days off as he wanted and retain all the profits from his work.

But nobody told him that he also may have to work long and hard to meet deadlines, manage his finances himself, and compete with thousands of others for the same clients.

It takes a special kind of person to work 60 hours a week for himself or herself so they don't have to work 40 hours a week for someone else.

Before venturing into this world, know that it is not all fun and games. Lots of serious thought must go into your actions if you are to be successful. Having thought it over and feeling sure that freelancing or consulting is right for you, it is time to start looking for work. Be absolutely certain not to violate any agreements you might have with a current employer.

Do not quit your job straight away as you will not have a livable source of income for a few months, at least, while searching for paying projects.

A first step should be to log onto your computer, pull open your web browser of choice, head over to one of the top three search engines, and start looking.

Use specific keywords to describe what you want and you should wind up with a massive database of different websites that cater to the freelance community in your field.

Once you have constructed a list of the top websites where clients are likely to be found visit the sites daily (or subscribe to them) to find projects that would not only be interesting but pay the bills.

As time passes, and you amass clients, more and more people will hear of you and the kind of work you do.

In this way you can attract the higher paying projects that will really supplement your income.

Eventually potential clients may come to you because of your good reputation. Word of mouth referrals are one of the most powerful marketing tools available.

It's important to create a mass of different items that can showcase your work. A portfolio may be critical to your success as a freelancer.

Include only the projects for which you retain full rights. If word gets around that someone thinks you may have stolen pieces of their portfolio, you risk damaging your reputation beyond repair and never attracting work. Add only projects that you actually complete.

Sure, if you are looking for freelance work as a web designer you *could* include an article you wrote on chemistry. But, why would someone looking for a skilled web designer care about something you wrote for a chemistry website, unless your client was also hiring you to write his web copy?

Finally, competition from around the globe is another barrier to self-sufficiency. Prepare to offer something that the competition simply cannot compete with and at much lower price points.

For example, noting a native tongue, such as English or French, for a freelance writer or editor, can be a plus. Ease of communication could be a big selling point for clients in many countries.

Graphic and web designers as well as software programmers should take plenty of extra courses, both in and out of college to illustrate how well they are educated in their craft.

Finally, no matter what your field take the time to create additions to your portfolio that highlight your strong points.

Where to Look for Customers

Not so long ago the best route for a freelancer to a potentially high paying client was solely through residents and local businesses in the community.

It was easier for writers, rather than web designers or software programmers, due to the large number of magazines and newspapers that traditionally needed constant freelance contributions.

Thanks to the Internet, finding work has never been easier. Individuals and companies always need freelancers for a project or two. They can help you get started and hopefully you might be lucky enough to find a client that wants to work with you time and time again.

A freelancer can also use the internet to market services on various forums and other freelance websites. In this way prospective clients come to you while you work on other projects.

Getting your name out there is an important first step. Let everyone know who you are, what you do, how well you do it, and where they can get in contact with you.

Potential clients love a freelancer who is willing to get the job done right the first time and fast. Finding clients in masses requires targeting various forums and discussion boards that dot the web.

Using Google is a great way to search for different websites that are specific to your chosen freelance field. Don't post advertisements on forums not frequented by people in your line of work. Posting out of section could result in you being banned.

Because it is important to focus on freelance websites directed to your field of operation, chose one or two services where you might find freelance work and go from there.

It is much easier to find work online as a writer, editor, photographer, web designer, or software programmer because there are many different freelance directories available.

One of the best places to start – for any type of freelancer – is craigslist, www.craigslist.com. This is a one-stop shop that lists jobs, both full-time and part-time "gigs", in metropolitan areas as well as in cities and countries. Most of the jobs offered on craigslist allow remote working from home although visits to offices in some of the higher paying positions may be necessary occasionally.

Additionally, build a list of potential customers using Fiverr, at www.fiverr.com. It's a site where people offer nearly anything for a mere $5. For example, one advertisement in the writing and editing category began with this title: *I will proofread your college essay for grammar and spelling up to 1,000 words.* Another stated this: *I will proofread any 2000 word text in Romanian for $5.* Yet another offered: *I will proofread* *and edit up to 500 words for $5*. Which freelancer would you choose?

These smaller, up front jobs up may help gain the trust of customers who return for repeat business. Another amazing resource for freelancers of all kinds is Guru, www.guru.com, a website that helps prospective freelancers in all fields find customers from around the world. It caters mostly to established freelance professionals though, so you may want to turn to it once you have exhausted other consulting options.

There are several excellent consulting websites for freelance writers and editors. One of them is Freelance Writing: www.freelancewriting.com. This is a massive database where employers and freelancers post information to find suitable matches for individual projects. Although catering to mostly lower paying jobs, it is a great start for your first consult or if you are looking simply for a couple of easy part-time projects to supplement your current income. As one of the leading websites also for those involved in programming and design, it is probably the most likely place to find a well paid job in the web and software field.

Among other website resource options is Freelance Job Search, www.freelancejobsearch.com a website that posts lesser known, but better paying freelance jobs in web design, graphic design, and programming. Designers and programmers could also turn to Script Lance, now www.freelancer.com, as a source of new leads.

The Writer's Market, www.writersmarket.com is also a site, not only to find work but to check out all the ins and outs of the writing and editing business. Get in touch with potential clients as well as hone your skills.

These resources are a great start in your freelancing or consulting efforts. Pretty soon by working for yourself and diversifying your income, you'll be more connected and passionate about your work as well as less dependent on any one person or organization.

Sample Contractor/Consultant Agreement

Company Logo   Company Name
Address
Email address

CONSULTANT/SUBCONTRACTOR AGREEMENT

This Consultant/Subcontractor Agreement ("this Agreement") is made and entered into as of _____ by and between COMPANY X, LLC ("COMPANY X"), a Virginia limited liability company, _____having an address at_____ and a _____ corporation (if applicable) having a place of business at _____("Consultant"). COMPANY X and Consultant desire to enter into an agreement whereby Consultant will provide certain services to, and perform certain work for, COMPANY X. The parties hereto agree as follows:

DEFINITIONS:

"Consultant" means the individual specified above.

"Firm, Fixed Price" or "FFP" shall mean one price to provide certain specified and described Services.

"Hourly Fee" or T&M" shall mean a fixed rate per hour paid for all Services provided, with additional expenses or materials paid for at "cost" or at "cost plus a handling charge."

"Services" means, as the context requires, the services to be performed by Consultant hereunder.

"Task Order(s)" means that document issued with reference to this Agreement which describes the Services to be provided by the Consultant when and as ordered by COMPANY X.

"Work Product" means, as the context requires, any software, ideas, concepts, techniques, inventions, processes, writings or works of authorship developed, created and/or provided by Consultant during the course of performing the Services and embodied, in whole or in part, in Consultant's deliverable(s) to COMPANY X or to a COMPANY X client.

COMPENSATION AND PAYMENT:
(a) COMPANY X agrees to pay Consultant for performance of Services in accordance with the Task Orders issued under this Agreement. A labor rate, applicable to all Task Orders unless otherwise stated in the Task Order, is specified in Exhibit B, attached hereto. If an hourly rate is specified, Consultant's time shall be computed to the nearest one quarter of an hour; and, if a daily rate is specified, a day shall consist of not less than eight hours of work. If an estimated cost for a Time and Material or Labor Hour rate agreement is specified on a Task Order, Consultant shall not exceed the estimated cost without prior written approval of COMPANY X. Further, COMPANY X will not pay Consultant in excess of the estimated cost of a Task Order without prior written approval.

(b) Consultant shall invoice COMPANY X based on work actually performed under a Task Order either (i) within seven working days after the end of each calendar month during which work was performed; or (ii) when compensation is due and payable in accordance with a specific Task Order. Such invoice shall specify the Task Order number, address to which payment shall be submitted, the hourly or daily rate and the hours or days actually worked if a Task Order is performed on a Time and Materials basis, and other relevant information.

(c) Provided Consultant's invoice and supporting documentation are acceptable, payment of Consultant's invoice will be made by COMPANY X within fifteen (15) days of COMPANY X's receipt of payment by its client(s), if Consultant's work was performed specifically for one COMPANY X client. Otherwise, COMPANY X will pay within thirty (30) days of invoice receipt. The Consultant will submit its invoices to COMPANY X via email to: email address or by regular mail to:

COMPANY X, LLC
Address

(d) If authorized in advance of expenditure, Consultant will be reimbursed for all reasonable and necessary expenses incurred in the course of business for travel outside of the greater metropolitan area of Consultant's principle place of business. Greater metropolitan area shall mean at a radius of more than 50 miles from Consultant's place of business. Consultant is not entitled to any advances for travel expenses. Consultant shall not be reimbursed for any mileage, parking fees, meals and similar expenses for travel within a 50 mile radius of Consultant's principle place of business, unless such reimbursement has been specified in a Task Order.
(1) Consultant shall obtain air travel at the least expensive rate available consistent with meeting the travel requirements of providing the Services in a reasonable timeframe. Unless otherwise authorized, meal, hotel and private automobile expenses shall not exceed the amounts specified on Exhibit B.
(2) Consultant shall complete an expense report form, and provide supporting receipts for all expenditures except for meals under $25.00. Such expense reports shall be submitted to COMPANY X within three business days of the conclusion of such travel.

(e) Nothing herein shall be deemed to constitute a waiver of COMPANY X's right to dispute and refuse to pay, in whole or in part, claims for compensation or reimbursable expenses if Consultant has materially misrepresented his or her capacity to perform an accepted assignment, failed to substantially accomplish satisfactorily the results specified, or otherwise materially breached any provision of this Agreement.

TERM:

This Agreement will become effective on the date first set forth above and shall continue in twelve (12) month increments unless written notice is provided by either party sixty (60) days prior to the end of the then-current twelve (12) month period, or until terminated in accordance with the "Termination" clause. The term of each Task Order will be stated in the Task Order and such term shall run independently of the term of this Agreement.

SERVICES:
Consultant agrees to provide the type of Services set forth in Exhibit A as and when specifically ordered under Task Orders referencing this Agreement. COMPANY X may, at any time, increase or decrease the scope of the Services and/or Work Product specifically ordered under a Task Order, provided that any change requiring additional services shall be subject to the parties' mutual agreement regarding Consultant's compensation in connection therewith. Any such agreement regarding additional compensation shall be set forth in a signed, written amendment to the relevant Task Order.

TASK ORDERS:
As stated under the clause entitled "Services," all work under this Agreement shall be ordered by Task Orders. A sample Task Order form may be found in Exhibit C. Each Task Order shall be bilaterally executed and shall state, at a minimum, the following information:

(a) the type of contractual arrangement for the individual Task Order—e.g., Firm, Fixed Price (FFP), Time and Materials (T&M) etc.;
(b) the Statement of Work for the Task Order;
(c) the Period of Performance for the Task Order;
(d) the price(s) for the work to be performed;
(e) the payment schedule, if applicable, for the work to be performed;
(f) that the Task Order is issued under the terms of this Agreement; and
(g) any special terms and conditions for the Task Order, including the incorporation of COMPANY X's client terms and conditions, if applicable.

Each Task Order shall be treated as a part of this Agreement but shall be severable and segregable from this Agreement with respect to the term of the Task Order, the price or estimated cost, the payment amount, the Statement of Work (SOW), any additional Special Terms and Conditions and any other similar terms which would clearly be applicable only to the specific Task Order in which those terms appear. If this Agreement is terminated in accordance with the "Termination" clause or the "Term" clause, this Agreement shall not be considered terminated in its entirety until the end of the period of performance of each and every Task Order which was not specifically terminated by the termination notice.

METHOD OF PERFORMANCE AND SUPERVISION:
Consultant will generally determine the method, details and means of performing the Services. COMPANY X shall not have the right to control the exact manner or determine the precise method of accomplishing the Services; however, COMPANY X shall be entitled to exercise a broad, general right of supervision and control over the results of the Services performed to ensure satisfactory performance. This power of supervision shall include the right to inspect, stop work, make suggestions or recommendations as to the details of the work, and request modifications to the scope of the Services.

SCHEDULING AND REPORTING:
Requirements for written reports, if any, shall be specified in the individual Task Orders.

PLACE OF WORK:
Consultant will perform the Services at Consultant's own office or work site unless otherwise designated on the individual Task Order.

RIGHT TO REJECT:
COMPANY X reserves the right, in its sole reasonable discretion, to reject the Services, and Consultant agrees that he/she shall immediately cease any work under this Agreement if such a rejection occurs. Reasons for rejection may include, but are not limited to, poor performance, threatening behavior, intoxication, drug use and similar behaviors which might impair the timely and professional provision of Services under this Agreement.

NON-EXCLUSIVE RELATIONSHIP:
This Agreement is non-exclusive. Consultant shall retain the right to perform work for other parties during the term of this Agreement, and COMPANY X may have work of the same or a similar kind performed by its own personnel or

other contractors or consultants during the term of this Agreement.

CONFLICT OF INTEREST:
Consultant will report to COMPANY X during the term of this Agreement about any and all contracts, agreements, understandings, prior employment or prior relationships applicable to Consultant, which may prohibit, restrict or limit Consultant's performance of this Agreement.

INDEPENDENT CONTRACTOR STATUS:
The parties hereto acknowledge and agree that Consultant is an independent contractor to COMPANY X and not an employee, agent, joint venturer or partner of COMPANY X. Consultant further acknowledges and agrees that, as an independent contractor, Consultant will not be entitled to (1) make a claim for unemployment, worker's compensation or disability pursuant to this Agreement or Consultant's relationship with COMPANY X, or (2) receive any vacation, health, retirement or other benefits pursuant to this Agreement or Consultant's relationship with COMPANY X. COMPANY X will not (a) withhold FICA from its payments to Consultant, (b) make state or federal unemployment insurance contributions on behalf of Consultant, or (c) withhold state and federal income taxes from its payments to Consultant. Consultant hereby represents and warrants to COMPANY X that, except as otherwise expressly provided herein, all activities and work performed by Consultant under this Agreement shall be at Consultant's own risk and liability. Consultant's taxpayer identification number and local business license/permit number, if applicable, are set forth on Exhibit B.

INTELLECTUAL PROPERTY:
(a) COMPANY X owns all rights, title and interest in all Work Products provided by Consultant under this Agreement, including but not limited to all copyrights, trade secrets and other forms of intellectual property rights, and all Work Products shall be deemed "works made for hire." To the extent that any such Work Product may not be considered a "work made for hire" under applicable law, Consultant hereby grants, transfers, assigns and conveys to COMPANY X and COMPANY X's clients an exclusive, paid-up, worldwide, perpetual license to 1) use, execute, reproduce, display, perform, distribute (internally and externally) copies of, and prepare derivative works based upon, such Work Product and derivative works thereof, and 2) authorize others to do any, some or all of the foregoing, such that COMPANY X and COMPANY X's clients may use and copy the Work Product and/or create derivative works from the Work Product unencumbered in any fashion by claims from the Consultant or a third party of the Consultant's and/or a third party's rights, title or interest in the Work Product or its underlying intellectual property.

(b) Consultant shall be free to use and employ its general skills, know-how and expertise, and to use, disclose and employ any generalized ideas, concepts, inventions, manuals, software, data files, know-how, methods, techniques or skills gained or learned during the course of the performance of any Services, so long as Consultant acquires and applies such information without the disclosure of any Proprietary Information and without any unauthorized use or disclosure of any Work Product. All ideas, concepts, inventions, manuals, software, data files, know-how, methods, techniques, skills and other intellectual property that Consultant has developed, created or acquired outside of performing the Services under this Agreement are and shall remain the sole and exclusive proprietary property of Consultant, except to the extent that rights are granted to COMPANY X and COMPANY X's clients as described in this clause.

WARRANTIES:
Consultant warrants that: (1) any and all representations made in resumes and other written or oral presentations to COMPANY X relating to Consultant's education, training, skills, work experience and similar matters are true and accurate; (2) all Services will be performed by Consultant utilizing the standards of care normally and customarily exercised by a professional performing comparable services under similar conditions; (3) Consultant has all requisite right and authority to enter into this Agreement with COMPANY X and that by doing so Consultant will not create any conflict of interest of any type, and should such conflict of interest later arise, shall provide COMPANY X with immediate notice of any such conflict of interest; (4) Consultant has no knowledge of any claims that would adversely affect Consultant's ability to assign all right, title and interest in and to the Work Product to COMPANY X; (5) the Work Product does not violate any patent, copyright or other proprietary right of any third party; and (6) Consultant has the legal right to grant COMPANY X the assignment of Consultant's interest in the Work Product as set forth in this Agreement.

INSURANCE:
Consultant shall obtain and maintain in full force and effect during the term of this Agreement (1) commercial general liability insurance (including contractual liability coverage) with coverage limits of not less than Five Hundred Thousand ($500,000) per occurrence; (2) auto liability insurance with coverage limits of not less than One Million Dollars ($1,000,000) per occurrence; and (3) worker's compensation insurance as, and if, required by law.

Consultant shall provide COMPANY X with a certificate of insurance evidencing the insurance coverages required under this clause when requested.

INDEMNIFICATION:
To the fullest extent permitted by law, Consultant shall indemnify, defend and hold COMPANY X and COMPANY X's clients harmless from and against any and all claims, demands, actions, suits proceedings, losses, damages, penalties, obligations, liabilities, costs and expenses (including, without limitation, reasonable attorneys' fees) arising directly or indirectly, in whole or in part from the negligence or willful misconduct of Consultant or the breach by Consultant of its obligations under this Agreement (including, without limitation, the breach of any warranty set forth under the clause entitled, "Warranty,") except to the extent arising from the sole negligence or willful misconduct of COMPANY X.

TERMINATION:
(a) Termination for Convenience
This Agreement may be terminated at any time in whole or in part for the convenience of COMPANY X by providing the Consultant with prior written notice. Such notice shall specify the extent to which the Agreement is being terminated, including which, and to what extent, current Task Orders are being terminated. Upon receipt of such notice, Consultant shall cease providing further Services as of the date of termination specified in the notice, advise COMPANY X of the extent to which Consultant has completed the Services through such termination date, and deliver to COMPANY X whatever Work Product then exists, and any physical embodiment thereof, in the manner requested by COMPANY X. COMPANY X shall make a final settlement payment to Consultant for all work performed through the date of such termination based on actual hours worked and actual expenses incurred if the work is being performed on a time and materials basis, or on a percent of completion if performed on a firm, fixed price basis.

(b) Termination for Default
(a) If either party fails to cure any breach of its obligations under this Agreement within ten (10) days following written notice from the other party, then such other party may terminate all or part of this Agreement, effective immediately, by providing the defaulting party with written notice of termination. Such written notice of termination shall specify the extent to which individual Task Orders are being terminated.

(b) If Consultant becomes bankrupt or otherwise insolvent, COMPANY X may, at its sole option and with written notice effective immediately, terminate this Agreement for default and pursue any other remedies available at law or in equity.

EXERCISE OF RIGHTS:
COMPANY X's failure to exercise any of its rights shall not constitute a waiver of any past, present or future right or remedy.

SURRENDER OF COMPANY X MATERIALS, DOCUMENTS, AND EQUIPMENT:
Upon the earlier of: (1) the termination of this Agreement, (2) the completion of a Task Order, or (3) a written demand by COMPANY X, Consultant shall promptly return to COMPANY X or to COMPANY X clients, as directed by COMPANY X, all documents, writings, tools, equipment and other materials made available to Consultant by COMPANY X and/or COMPANY X clients, or compiled or generated by Consultant in the course of performing Services hereunder, all of which shall be deemed to be the property of COMPANY X and/or its clients.

PROPRIETARY INFORMATION:
All proprietary, confidential and business information of COMPANY X and/or its clients including, but not limited to, information in tangible form marked with "Proprietary," "Confidential" or similar markings, specifications, processes, procedures, written documents, source code, capabilities, current or prospective products, services, customers or contracts, marketing strategies, research and development activities, and financial data ("Proprietary Information") shall be protected by the Consultant from disclosure to third parties. Any and all Proprietary Information shall be protected in the same manner and to the same degree that the Consultant protects its own proprietary information, but at a minimum will not: (1) disclose such Proprietary Information to any person unless authorized by COMPANY X in writing; (2) directly or indirectly use such Proprietary Information for Consultant's benefit or for that of any other business; and (3) will do all things reasonably required or requested by COMPANY X and/or COMPANY X's clients for the protection of such Proprietary Information. Consultant may use or disclose Proprietary Information that is or becomes publicly available, is already lawfully in Consultant's possession, is independently developed by Consultant, is lawfully obtained from third parties or the disclosing party has granted prior and specific written consent to the Consultant indicating the Proprietary Information may be disclosed to a third party.

Protection of any such Proprietary Information shall continue for a period of seven (7) years following the termination of this Agreement in accordance with the "Termination" clause or the "Term" clause, as appropriate. The provisions of this clause shall survive the termination of this Agreement.

EXCUSED PERFORMANCE:
Neither party shall be liable for, and is excused from any failure to deliver or perform or for delay in delivery or performance due to causes beyond its reasonable control, including but not limited to, acts of nature, governmental actions, acts of war, fire, flood, labor difficulties, shortages, civil disturbances, transportation problems, interruptions of power or communications, or failure of suppliers.

NO HIRE:
In the event Consultant incorporates as a business entity and/or becomes capable of hiring staff, Consultant agrees not to hire, or to solicit for hire, any COMPANY X staff, including COMPANY X's other consultants, either as employees or contractors, during the term of this Agreement and for a period of one (1) year following the termination of this Agreement, without the prior written consent of COMPANY X. In addition, the Consultant agrees that during the term of this Agreement and for a period of one (1) year after the conclusion of a specific task order, Consultant will not accept the same work performed under a Task Order either directly or indirectly from COMPANY X's client, without the prior written consent of COMPANY X.

ASSIGNMENT OR TRANSFER:
Neither party to this Agreement may assign or transfer its interest in this Agreement to any other entity without prior written consent of the other party.

MODIFICATIONS:
Any modifications of this Agreement shall be in writing and executed by both COMPANY X and the Consultant.

AUDIT:
To the extent that actual costs or labor hours of personnel form the basis of payment under this Agreement, the Consultant shall provide to COMPANY X supporting documentation which is adequate to perform audit and verification of such actual costs and labor hours.

ORDER OF PRECEDENCE:
In the event of an inconsistency in this Agreement, unless otherwise provided herein, the inconsistency shall be resolved by giving precedence in the following order:

(a) Task Order's Price, Payment and Statement of Work Clauses
(b) This Agreement
(c) Other terms and conditions added to a Task Order
(d) Terms and conditions from a COMPANY X client contract incorporated by reference in a Task Order

APPLICABLE LAW:
This Agreement shall be governed by the laws of the Commonwealth of Virginia (Note: tailor to your particular region and laws).

IN WITNESS WHEREOF, THE PARTIES HAVE EXECUTED THIS AGREEMENT AS OF THE LAST DATE WRITTEN BELOW:

Consultant
Name of Business:		Date:

Signature:

Printed Name:

Title:

EIN or SSN:

COMPANY X
Name of Business:	COMPANY X, LLC Date: December			3,			2012

Signature:
Printed Name:
John Doe

Title:

Company Logo   COMPANY X
Address
Email

EXHIBIT A: Statement of Work
The Consultant shall perform the Services described below when and if ordered under this Agreement via Task Orders:

1. Service Type
    Service Description

EXHIBIT B: Prices/Rates/Other Info

(a) The following labor rate shall be applicable to all work ordered under this Agreement: $0/hour

(b) Meals while in travel status shall be reimbursed at actual cost not to exceed a total of: $0/day

(c) Hotel expenses while in travel status shall be reimbursed at actual cost not to exceed: $0/day

(d) Mileage for Consultant's use of a personal car on behalf of COMPANY X business: $0/day

Company Logo   COMPANY X
Address
Email

EXHIBIT C: Sample Task Order

This Task Order is issued under the COMPANY X, LLC Consultant Agreement effective _____
between COMPANY X and:

Consultant Name:
Address:

Task Order No:
Task Order Type: T&M (or FFP)
Period of Performance: 00/00/0000 - 00/00/0000
Labor Rates: (If applicable, see Exhibit B)
Total Price or Total Estimated Cost: $
Payment Schedule (FFP only and if applicable):

Statement of Work:

Special Terms and Conditions Applicable Only to this Order:

(If the Special Terms and Conditions listed above include terms and conditions from a COMPANY X client, such terms and conditions shall be interpreted to read as follows: the name of the COMPANY X client shall mean "COMPANY X ," and the words "Contractor," "Supplier," "Vendor," "Consultant" or similar words shall mean the Consultant as defined in the main body of this Agreement. Any Special Terms and Conditions shall be applicable only to this Task Order and shall not apply to any other Task Order or to this Agreement as a whole unless specifically so stated.)

Consultant		COMPANY X	
Name of Business:	Date:	Name of Business:	Date:

Chris Lutz

Signature: Signature:

Printed Name: Printed Name:

Title: Title:

Working at Home: Time is of the Essence

The main reason some say they want to work at home is because they work only when they want to work. It is true that you can set your own work hours at home but it does not mean that you don't need set work hours.

A 'hit or miss' work schedule – a lack of any work schedule at all – simply will not work. Time is of the Essence! YOUR time!

Working at home can be a very, very good thing. You see the kids off to school and are there when they get home. You can put on a load of laundry and work while it runs through the cycles. You can schedule medical, dental and other appointments or pick up kids from day camps during vacations. Dinner can be cooked well before a flock of hungry buzzards descends.

It can also be a very, very bad thing if you can't plan your time well or don't set up a work schedule that you and your family can operate in. When you work at home, despite the automatic perks, time management is essential.

Inefficiency – spending too much time accomplishing tasks – could lead to failure on the work or home front. Not only must you establish a work schedule, it needs to be enforced you, your family and friends as well. Many women, in particular, who work from home are often interrupted with phone calls from family members when they need to be working.

A job in the brick and mortar world provides:

1. Structure for your day
2. A signal to family and friends that your time is spoken for during working hours.

Notice that both these benefits provided by a regular job relate to your TIME.

First, let's discuss the structure a regular job provides and how it can be applied to your work-at-home job or business. A job outside the home requires your presence during a specified time on specified days of the week. Working from home needs the same kind of structure, in particular a set number of regular working hours. You can choose the hours ... but you do have to choose!

Now, let's talk about your family and friends and how they view your work-at-home job. It is a strange but true fact that your dear mother would not dream of calling you at your 'real' job to ask you to drive Aunt Rosie to the beauty salon and wait until she is finished. After all, you are working and can't be expected to leave your job to run errands. Right?

That very same considerate mother will call and ask you to transport Aunt Rosie to and from the salon when you work from home. Why? Because you are at home and available.

Your dear, sweet mother will not view your work-at-home job as a 'real' job. Your spouse will see you as being free to run errands. And friends will want you to be available for long telephone conversations, lunch, or for a coffee klatch.

You can see the problem. If you do not schedule your time and abide by your schedule yourself, others will not. Unless you see your work-at-home job as a real job with real working hours, your time will be eaten up. You will not be able to finish anything.

You will fail and find yourself looking for a real job unless you view your work at home job as the real thing with regular working hours that make you unavailable for other activities.

The best way to accomplish this is to set a schedule and inform your family and friends what it is. You don't have to be rude but you do have to be firm. Make it clear to all. Pin up a note.

"I will be working between 9 am and 3 pm Monday through Friday. On those days and during those hours, I am not available to run errands or take personal phone calls or entertain company." Then stick to it!

For work-at-home entrepreneurs time is their single most valuable asset. Nothing can replace time – valuable, precious time!

No matter how rich or poor you are, no matter how many things are on your 'to-do' list, there are still only 24 hours in each day.

But we can't spend all of them working. We have to sleep, eat and shower. Family and friends also require some of our time. Relationships must be nurtured, not neglected. We can allow ourselves just so many work hours each day. Since our working time is limited that means we must make the very most of the hours we work. We can't waste time on unimportant details or on tasks that others can do.

When you shave a few minutes here and a few minutes there, you will make more efficient use of your allotted work hours. Here are a few suggestions.

Email Account Efficiency

We all have various email accounts. One is for this and another is for that. Checking every email account more than once a day can be time-consuming but shortened by having all email delivered into one gmail account. Additionally, don't spend time reading and answering emails that don't add to your bottom line.

Email comes in several varieties. There are emails that are business-related, emails that are important but not business-related and emails that are simply frivolous and time wasting. If an email has been forwarded several times, don't waste your time.

If an email is addressed to a great many people, don't waste time on it either. Email can consume a lot of time. You need to filter the important from the irrelevant and only spend time on those emails that are related to your business.

Set Up Time Tables to Help Prioritize Your Work Day

A scheduled work day is an efficient work day. You will accomplish more in less time if you know in advance, and can see at a glance, what task is next. A timetable is a visual aid. It can help you allot your time efficiently and productively.

Focus on Result-Producing Activities

When you make your work day schedule, be certain that the tasks will, in fact, make your business thrive. Don't waste time, effort and energy on tasks that can be done by others. Investigate outsourcing and add hours to your day by sending mundane business tasks to others.

You can outsource bookkeeping and accounting, article and ebook submissions, travel and event planning and ad writing. Others may be able to perform these tasks better and more efficiently. Your time is better spent growing your business, making those contacts and closing those deals!

Shave Time on Counter-Productive Activities

Your friends and families demand some of your time but you can also waste a lot on unproductive activities like watching TV. Keep a record of what you do over several days and you'll be surprised at how much of your day is wasted.

Of course, we all need down time. We must relax our minds and bodies. We can't be all business all the time, but we can limit our unproductive or counterproductive activities. Time is precious and limited. We need to make the best use of every minute.

Outsourcing: How to Get More Done in Less Time

Time equals money. You are an entrepreneur. Ask yourself about the best use of your time because it is your time that equals money. The health of your bottom line is directly affected by the way you choose to allot your working hours.

Your job as an entrepreneur is to grow your business, to make those contacts that will make you money. Your job is to conceive ideas and bring them to fruition. Your job is to close that deal!

Okay! Now for what your job as an entrepreneur is not. It does not qualify you as an accountant, an advertising guru or a writer. You aren't qualified to be an event planner or a travel agent. When you decided to build a modular career and become an entrepreneur it did not automatically make you a "jack-of-all-trades."

You can waste a lot of valuable time on tasks that you aren't very good at. You are the idea man/woman. You'll be good at making your business grow if that is where you use your time and direct your energies.

Doing it all yourself, whether you are good at it or not, will use up all thought and energy leaving nothing for what only you can do to make your business grow. The 80/20 rule is likely to be at work here too. Remember to focus only on the 20 per cent that brings you the most revenue and outsource the rest or as much as you can.

Accountant or Bookkeeping Service

Every business must keep a record of its day-to-day financial transactions. The smallest of transactions can add up to big tax deductions over a year. You can't simply file everything under 'miscellaneous' spend even an hour every day attending to mundane bookkeeping duties either. Bookkeepers and accountants charge only for the time that they spend working for you. Usually they have many clients. It's easy to make use of their services. In fact, some never meet their bookkeepers because they work completely virtually.

If a bookkeeper spends an hour working on your records then you will charged for that one hour. You aren't a bookkeeper or an accountant so you may spend three or four hours on the same tasks, with questionable results. Hire an accountant or a bookkeeping service – particularly if they charge $40 per hour and you can make $60 per hour doing what you do best. It's a no-brainer.

Hire a VA (Virtual Assistant)

You don't have to do all of it yourself. You can scale up your venture by replicating yourself, hiring more people, or outsourcing tasks that do not produce much revenue. Virtual assistants are a great resource for your side business.

They can work from anywhere in the world. A great site is http://www.onlinejobs.ph. It matches you with appropriate virtual assistant candidates who speak clear English. And the pay rates are inexpensive for full-time virtual work. Many cost about $200-300 a month! They have a special section for pre-found, tested and scored professionals with their resumes compiled so that you can link with the right assistant. Having others work virtually can bring financial advantages and allow you to make the most of your time. A virtual assistant can save hours of time on mundane tasks that are necessary for a successful business. They can check and filter your emails so only the most vital need your response. Internet entrepreneurs get more junk mail than anybody! A good VA can also act as a travel agent and make airline and hotel reservations.

Ghost Writers and Article Submission Services

Ghost writers will post to blogs and forums above your own signature file that includes your name and website. Some ghost writers will also submit articles and ebooks for you. If the ghost writer that you employ does not, then you can seek an articles submission company for that time-consuming task.

Advertising Agencies

These do not come cheap so be specific about what you need. You may get pay per click advertisements written rather reasonably – which is a huge help.

CONCLUSION

I sincerely hope that you've enjoyed this book. I hope that you've learned something worthwhile here and are able to implement it for yourself. I hope this instills a sense of clarity and organization that can allow you to go forward in an efficient manner.

Entrepreneurship is a journey. Most of us have chosen it as a lifestyle. Many of us won't make it. Not on our first try anyway. It's important that we try to help and support each other. It's a frightening world for us some times. And, like I said at the beginning, some of us pay a real price for choosing this lifestyle.

It's important that you don't give up. Manage your energy well. Try not to burn out. Be shrewd, be effective, be productive, and be efficient.

Do what you have to do. If you have to work another job while building your business, do that. Almost no one is an overnight success. It can be the biggest challenge of our lives. It is for me. But, the potential rewards and pay off can be unlimited.

Stay strong, stay focused on why you do what you do. If you're like me and on this journey too, living this lifestyle, I'm a fan. Keep up the good work. Be sure to connect with the rest of us who are like you and we'll all continue to support each other. Thanks for reading and thanks for continuing to do all that you do.

To send you off on the right foot, I'll leave you with the top 50 success quotes of all time. Enjoy!

1. "Identify your problems but give your power and energy to solutions." Tony Robbins

2. "You live longer once you realize that any time spent being unhappy is wasted." Ruth E. Renkl

3. "The only true wisdom is knowing that you know nothing." Socrates

4. "Things work out best for those who make the best of how things work out." John Wooden

5. "Let no feeling of discouragement prey upon you, and in the end you are sure to succeed." Abraham Lincoln

6. " If you are not willing to risk the usual you will have to settle for the ordinary." Jim Rohn

7. "Trust because you are willing to accept the risk, not because it's safe or certain." Anonymous

8. "When your life flashes before your eyes, make sure you've got plenty to watch." Anonymous

9. "Screw it, Let's do it!" Richard Branson

10. "Be content to act, and leave the talking to others." Baltasa

11. "Innovation distinguishes between a leader and a follower." Steve Jobs

12. "The more you loose yourself in something bigger than yourself, the more energy you will have." Norman Vincent Peale

13. "If your ship doesn't come in, swim out to meet it!" Jonathan Winters

14. "People often say that motivation doesn't last. Well, neither does bathing – that's why we recommend it daily." Zig Ziglar

15. "Courage is being scared to death, but saddling up anyway." John Wayne

16. "Too many of us are not living our dreams because we are living our fears." Les Brown

17. "The link between my experience as an entrepreneur and that of a politician is all in one word: freedom." Silvio Berlusconi

18. "The entrepreneur builds an enterprise; the technician builds a job." Michael Gerber

19. "A real entrepreneur is somebody who has no safety net underneath them." Henry Kravis

20. "Most new jobs won't come from our biggest employers. They will come from our smallest. We've got to do everything we can to make entrepreneurial dreams a reality." Ross Perot

21. "My son is now an 'entrepreneur'. That's what you're called when you don't have a job." Ted Turner

22. "As we look ahead into the next century, leaders will be those who empower others." Bill Gates

23. "As long as you're going to be thinking anyway, think big." Donald Trump

24. "If you want to achieve excellence, you can get there today. As of this second, quit doing less-than-excellent work." Thomas J Watson

25. "Opportunity is missed by most people because it is dressed in overalls and looks like work." Thomas Edison

26. "The only place where success comes before work is in the dictionary." Vidal Sassoon

27. "Capital isn't scarce; vision is." Sam Walton

28. "Failure defeats losers, failure inspires winners." Robert T. Kiyosaki

29. "Some people dream of great accomplishments, while others stay awake and do them." Anonymous

30. "I will tell you how to become rich. Close the doors. Be fearful when others are greedy. Be greedy when others are fearful." Warren Buffet

31. "Going into business for yourself, becoming an entrepreneur, is the modern-day equivalent of pioneering on the old frontier." Paula Nelson

32. "Poor people have big TV. Rich people have big library." Jim Rohn

33. "A goal is a dream with a deadline." Napoleon Hill

34. "Every day I get up and look through the Forbes list of the richest people in America. If I'm not there, I go to work." Vinnie Rege

35. "Expect the best. Prepare for the worst. Capitalize on what comes." Zig Ziglar

36. "People are not lazy. They simply have important goals – that is, goals that do not inspire them." Tony Robbins

37. "Nobody talks of entrepreneurship as survival, but that's exactly what it is." Anita Roddick

38. "The best reason to start an organization is to make meaning; to create a product or service to make the world a better place." Guy Kawasaki

39. "A friendship founded on business is a good deal better than a business founded on friendship." John D. Rockefeller

40. "I've been blessed to find people who are smarter than I am, and they help me to execute the vision I have." Russell Simmons

41. "I find that when you have a real interest in life and a curious life, that sleep is not the most important thing." Martha Stewart

42. "Logic will get you from A to B. Imagination will take you everywhere." Albert Einstein

43. "Success is liking yourself, liking what you do, and liking how you do it." Maya Angelou

44. "Success is walking from failure to failure with no loss of enthusiasm." Winston Churchill

45. "The function of leadership is to produce more leaders, not more followers." Ralph Nader

46. "Without continual growth and progress, such words as improvement, achievement, and success have no meaning." Benjamin Franklin

47. "Big pay and little responsibility are circumstances seldom found together." Napoleon Hill

48. Make your product easier to buy than your competition, or you will find your customers buying from them, not you." Mark Cuban

49. "The road to success and the road to failure are almost exactly the same." Colin R. Davis

50. "If you don't have a competitive advantage, don't compete." Jack Welch

And just as an added bonus, here are:

10 YouTube Videos about Entrepreneurs

1. http://youtu.be/VH35Iz9veM0 - Richard Branson: Advice for Entrepreneurs
2. http://youtu.be/zq4_Uf1jQE8 - Entrepreneurs Breakdowns and Breakthroughs
3. http://youtu.be/NcXiF4DZ8Hg - Introducing Google for Entrepreneurs
4. http://youtu.be/FTRnhp8uSVQ - Entrepreneurship --My Greatest Lesson from Four Years of Entrepreneurship
5. http://youtu.be/IhgEHTaVLiI - Kent Clothier: How To Be A Successful Entrepreneur
6. http://youtu.be/shXdZBKOCew - Two Generations of Entrepreneurship

7. http://youtu.be/ePiNfceCB8M - Taking On Challenges: How entrepreneurship drives America
8. http://youtu.be/Oo3qO-m1G-Q - How Entrepreneurs Can Unlock Creativity
9. http://youtu.be/7DtczfxXP6U - Michael Dell: Lessons For Entrepreneurial Success
10. http://youtu.be/HOXBgrVQgAw - 5 Tips Part-time Entrepreneurs Can Use to Achieve Full-time Success

ABOUT THE AUTHOR

Chris Lutz is an American entrepreneur living in the mid-Atlantic on the East coast. He's always wanted to be an entrepreneur and turn his interests and passions into businesses. He'd like to connect and become friends with other entrepreneurs from all industries.

Chris is founder and owner of the Sports Performance & Resistance Training Association (S.P.A.R.T.A.) with more than a decade of professional experience as a certified personal trainer.

His combination of BS degree in Exercise Science from George Mason University, a C.P.T certification, and over five years experience managing a training facility, earned him his Master Trainer status.

Chris is the author of several other books that can be found on Amazon.

His business, www.theentrepreneurlifestyle.com is a celebration of the lifestyle of entrepreneurs, from struggle to success with eBooks, tools, training, and other resources for entrepreneurs.

Chris' other business, www.lutzlures.com is an ecommerce site for the outdoor enthusiast, specifically kayak fishermen and hammock campers from which his own brand of lures and custom kayak fishing rods are available. He is a professional kayak fisherman, himself and provides guided trips locally on the Potomac river.